CHAMBERS
YOUNG SET
DICTIONARY
THREE

Amy L Brown
John Downing
John Sceats

Illustrations by Sostres

© W & R Chambers Ltd 1972
This edition 1976

Printed by T & A Constable Ltd, Edinburgh

ISBN 0 550 71197 X   school edition
ISBN 0 550 10618 9   trade edition

Preface

About this book

A dictionary is a list of words we can use. There are many different kinds of dictionaries, some of them very easy and some much more difficult. This one is the third of a graded series of four dictionaries for children. If you find it is too difficult, use *Dictionary Two*. If you are quite used to dictionaries, and this one does not have all the words you want, then go on to *Dictionary Four*.

The job of a dictionary is to tell us about words. A large dictionary for adults contains all the words people ever use and all their different meanings. It may also tell us where words come from and how they are pronounced. But the main use of any dictionary — and of this one — is to tell us what a word means if we don't know it, and how to spell it correctly.

The words in dictionaries are always arranged in alphabetical order, which means that there is only one right place for each word. You should be able to find the word you want very quickly, even in a large dictionary. If you are not good at this it is better to practise first on *Dictionaries One* and *Two*, until you are quick and sure.

How to find a word

Suppose you come across a word like **octopus** and want to know what it means. You know that **o** comes somewhere near the middle of the alphabet, so open the dictionary at the middle. You may be lucky and find **o** the first time. But if you find that all the words begin with **l** or **p** you have to ask yourself if **o** comes before or after. You will soon get very good at this.

Then look at the second letter of **octopus**, and find the words beginning **oc-**. Then, if you look at the third letter, you know that **octopus** comes after **ocean**, because **t** comes after **e**.

The letters above the line on the tops of the pages are the beginnings of the first and last words on those pages; they will save you looking through a lot of words before you have found the right page.

When you have found your word

After each word comes an explanation of what the word most often means. Sometimes there is a picture to help. Many words have quite a lot of different meanings, so test whether the one which is given makes sense in the sentence where you found the word. If it does not make sense at all there may be another meaning for the word which you could find in *Dictionary Four*.

If you don't understand some of the words used in the explanation, look them up too; you will find them in this dictionary.

It is sometimes interesting to look up words that you already know, to see if you agree with how the meaning is explained.

Are there any words in this Preface that you are not sure about? Why not try looking them up now?

To parents and teachers

Guidance on how best to use the *Young Set Dictionaries* with children will be found in *Words Children Want to Use*, the handbook to the series, which also contains an account of the research on which the series is based.

abacus a frame with beads on rods, used for
counting

abandon to go away forever from something or
somebody. The same word also means to stop
what you are doing before you have finished it.

abbess a woman who is the head of the nuns in a
convent or abbey

abbey a monastery or a convent; the big church of
a monastery or convent

abbot a man who is the head of the monks in a
monastery or abbey

abbreviation a short way of writing or printing a
word, such as Dr. for Doctor, Jan. for January

abdomen the lower part of the body which contains
the stomach

ability strength, cleverness or skill

able having the strength, cleverness or skill to do
something

abolish to get rid of or to put an end to something

above higher than; over

abroad away in another country

abrupt sudden; hurried

absent missing; away; not present

abundant more than enough; in great plenty

accent   tone of voice; a way of pronouncing words.
Londoners have a different accent from
people living in other parts of Britain.

accept   to agree to receive something

accident   something that happens by chance, usually
unpleasant

account   a statement of money owing or spent. The
same word also means an explanation.

accurate   correct; exactly right

accuse   to say someone has done something wrong

ace   a card, domino or die with one spot or mark

ache   a dull pain that goes on and on

acid   a liquid which can burn your skin. The same
word also means tasting sour or sharp.

acorn   the nut or seed that grows on an oak tree

acrobat   a person who does clever tricks, like
balancing on a rope at a circus

across   from one side to the other side of something

act   anything which is done is an act. The same
word also means to pretend you are someone
other than yourself, as in a play or film.

actor   a man or boy who acts in a play or film

action   something done; a series of acts performed

active   doing something; being busy or lively

actress   a woman or girl who acts in a play or film

actual   real; not imaginary

add   to put something together with something else. You add two and two to make four $(2+2=4)$.

addition   something added; the act of adding

additional   extra; added to something

address   the name and number of your house and the street and town where you are living. The same word also means to write or speak to people.

adenoids   two small fleshy lumps at the back of the nose

admiral   a very important officer in the navy

admire   to think very well of someone or something

admit   to agree that something is so. The same word means to allow someone to come in.

adult   a person who is fully grown-up

advance   to move forward

adventure   an exciting or dangerous thing that you do or that happens to you

aerial   the metal rods or wires which receive or send radio or television signals

aeroplane   a flying machine

affair   a happening or an event

affect   to do something that causes a change

affection   great liking; fondness

afford   to have enough money for something you want to buy

afloat floating on the water

afraid frightened; full of fear

after later; behind; following on

afternoon the time between midday and sunset

afterwards at a later time

again once more

against in an opposite direction to; on the opposite side to

age the number of years something or someone has been alive, or has existed

agile lively; nimble

agree to consent to something, or to think the same as someone else

agreeable friendly; easy to get on with

aground stuck on the sand or rocks. Ships sometimes run aground and cannot move without help.

ahead in front: before

aim to point a gun or other weapon steadily at the thing you want to hit

air the mixture of gases which we breathe and which surrounds the earth

aircraft any machine that can rise in the air and move through it

airfield a place where aircraft can land and take off

air force aircraft used for fighting and the people who control them

airgun a gun in which the bullet is shot by the force of compressed air

airman a man who flies or helps to fly aircraft

airport the place where aeroplanes come in to land and take off

airtight closed so tightly that air cannot get in or out

aisle a pathway between rows of seats in a church, a cinema or theatre

alarm sudden surprise or fear. The same word also means a warning of danger, often a bell.

album a book of blank pages in which you keep a collection of things like stamps or photographs

ale a kind of beer

alert wide awake; active or watchful

algebra a branch of mathematics in which you use letters as well as figures

alibi an excuse by someone that he could not have done something, because he can prove that he was somewhere else when it happened

alight in flames; burning

alive living; not dead

all the whole of; everything or everyone

alley a narrow passage between buildings in cities and towns

alligator a dangerous animal very like a crocodile, but with a shorter nose

allow   to permit or let

alloy   a mixture of two or more metals

all right   good; safe and sound; agreed

almanac   a book that gives information about the weather and other things that may happen in the days, weeks and months of one year

almond   a kind of flat nut that grows inside the fruit of an almond tree

almost   nearly, but not quite

alone   all by yourself; with nobody else

aloud   out loud; the opposite of silent

alphabet   all the letters used in a language, arranged in a special order

already   sooner than expected

alsatian   a large wolf-like dog

also   as well as; too; in addition

altar   a kind of raised table inside a church

alter   to make a change in something, to make or become different in some way

alteration   a change

although   even if; but; in spite of

aluminium   a lightweight, silver-coloured metal

always   at all times; forever

amateur   someone who plays games or takes part in something without being paid, because he likes doing it

amaze   to surprise greatly

ambition   a wish to do very well, or to have power

amble   to walk along slowly

ambulance   a special car for taking people who are ill or hurt to hospital

among   in the midst of

amount   a quantity; the sum reached when several things are added together

ample   of a large size; in plenty

amuse   to make others smile or laugh by something you say or do

anchor   a heavy iron hook which is attached to a ship by a chain. When it is thrown over the side, it digs into the sea bed and stops the ship from moving.

angel   a messenger from God

angle   the corner made when two lines meet at a point

angora   wool made from the long silky hair of the angora goat or rabbit

angry   very cross; in a bad temper

animal   any living creature which is not a plant

ankle   the thin bony part of your leg just above your foot

anniversary   a day which is remembered each year for something special which happened once, like a wedding anniversary

announce   to make something known by telling everyone

annoy   to make someone rather cross

anorak   a waterproof jacket, usually with a hood

another   one more; a different one

answer   anything said or written in reply, usually to a question

ant   a small insect

antarctic   at or around the South Pole

anthem   a piece of music sung by a church choir. The same word also means the national song of a country.

anti-clockwise   the opposite direction to the way clock hands move

anvil   an iron block on which pieces of metal can be hammered into shape

anxiety   worry; a feeling of fear about something you think might happen

anxious   worried or afraid about something you think might happen

anything   a thing of any kind

apart   not together

ape   a large monkey without a tail

apex   the highest tip of something, such as the top point of a triangle

apparatus   a collection of things that help you to do something, such as ropes and bars in a gymnasium

appeal   to ask for help

appear   to come into sight

appearance   the way someone or something looks to you; the coming into sight of someone or something

appetite   the desire to eat

applaud   to show you like some entertainment or performance by clapping your hands together

apple   a round red, green or yellow fruit which grows on a tree

approach   to go nearer to someone or something

approximate   nearly correct

apricot   a fruit which looks like a small yellow peach

apron   a piece of cloth which you tie around you to keep your clothes clean

aquarium   a container, usually a glass tank, where fish and other water animals are kept for people to look at

arc   a part of a circle, a curved line

arch   a part of something, usually a building, that is curved, such as the top of a doorway or window

archery   shooting at a target with bow and arrow

architect   someone who designs and plans buildings

arc-light   a lamp lit by an arc of electricity

arctic   at or around the North Pole; very cold

area   the extent of space on the ground or on a floor

arena   a large open space with seats all around, where you can watch games or sports

argue   to give reasons for or against something which is being discussed

argument   reasons for or against your opinion about something; a discussion

arise   to get up

arithmetic   working with numbers, like adding, subtracting, multiplying and dividing

ark   the houseboat which saved Noah and his family and the animals from drowning in the Flood. The same word also means a chest in which holy books are kept.

arm   the part of your body between your hand and your shoulder

armada   a great fleet of warships

armadillo   a small animal with an armour-like covering

armchair   a chair with sides on which to rest your arms

armour   a covering, usually made of metal, to protect the body in battle

armpit   the hollow place under the top part of your arm

arms war weapons, such as guns and cannons

army a large group of soldiers

around on all sides

arouse to wake someone or stir him into action

arrange to put in a special order

arrive to reach the place you set out for

arrow a thin straight stick made of wood with a sharp pointed tip. You shoot it with a bow.

art drawing, painting and sculpture. The same word is also used when something is done with great skill.

artful cunning; clever in a rather sneaky way

article a thing of a particular kind, such as an article of clothing. The same word also means a piece written in a newspaper or magazine.

artist a person who paints or draws pictures

ascend to go up; to move upward

ash the powdery stuff left when something has completely burned up

ashamed feeling shame

aside to one side; apart

ask to put a question to someone

asleep sleeping; not awake

aspirin a pain-killing medicine, usually in white tablets

ass a donkey, an animal rather like a small horse

assemble   to meet together, as when the whole
   school is called together for assembly

assist   to help

assistant   a helper; someone who serves in a shop

assorted   of many different kinds

astrologer   a fortune-teller who studies the stars

astrology   the study of the stars as a way of telling
   your fortune

astronaut   someone who travels
   in space

astronomer   a scientist who studies the stars and
   other bodies in the sky

astronomy   the scientific study of stars and other
   bodies in the sky

athlete   someone who is good at sports and games

atlas   a book of maps

atmosphere   the air that is around the earth

atom   an extremely small particle of anything

attach   to fasten, join or tie together

attack   to make a move to hurt someone or
   something

attempt   to try; to make an effort

attend   to be present. The same word also means
   to listen carefully to someone.

attendant a helper or servant in a public place, such as a car-park, theatre or cinema

attic a room just under the roof of a building

attract to make something or someone come nearer

attractive charming; lovely; having the power to make people want to be near you

auction a public sale where things are sold to the people who offer the most money for them

audience a group of people listening to or watching something like a play or a concert

aunt the sister of your father or mother

authority the power to control what other people do. The headmaster of a school has authority over the teachers and pupils.

autobiography the story of a person's life written by himself and not by someone else

automobile any vehicle with an engine, meant to be driven on the road

autumn the season between summer and winter, when the leaves fall

avenue a wide street or pathway, usually with trees on both sides

aviation the art of flying aircraft

aviator a pilot who flies an aircraft

avoid to escape; to keep out of the way of something

await to wait for or look for

awake   not asleep. You can hear and see what is going on around you.

award   to give someone something he has won, like a prize or medal

aware   knowing about something, as when you are aware of the danger of crossing a road with heavy traffic

away   not here or with you; absent

awe   great fear and wonder; great respect

awful   very bad, ugly or nasty

awkward   clumsy. The same word also means not convenient or not comfortable.

axe   a sharp tool with a long handle, used for chopping wood

axis   a real or imaginary line through the middle of an object, around which the object turns

axle   the long bar on a vehicle to which the wheels are attached

azalea   a shrub like a rhododendron, but smaller, with brightly coloured flowers

azure   a clear sky-blue colour

babble   to talk or make sounds in a foolish way: to make a murmuring sound as water does in a stream or brook

baboon   a large monkey with a short tail and a long dog-like face

baby   a very young child who cannot walk yet

babyish   like a baby

bachelor   a man who has not married

bacon   pigmeat that has been dried and salted

bad   not good; wrong; spoiled

badge   a special sign or mark you wear to show you belong to a certain school or club

badger   a grey, black and white striped animal which burrows in the earth with its long front claws

badminton   a game rather like tennis, in which you use a smaller racket and a shuttlecock

baffling   too hard or puzzling to understand

bag   a sack for holding things, often made of paper or plastic, but sometimes of leather or cloth

baggage   another word for luggage

bait   food used to attract fish or animals, so that they can be caught

bake   to cook in an oven

baker   a person who bakes and sells bread and cakes

balance   to hold something steady so that it does not tip or fall over

balcony   a platform, usually with railings or a low wall around it. It is built out from the side of a building.

bald   without any hair on the head

bale a specially packed bundle of something, like straw or cotton

ball an object which is completely round, often used for playing games. The same word also means a splendid dancing party.

ballerina a girl ballet dancer

ballet (*say balay*) a kind of dancing which tells a story in movement, with music, but without using words

balloon a bag filled with air or gas so that it can float above the ground

ballpoint a pen with a tiny ball instead of a point at the end

ballroom a very big room used for dancing

bamboo a kind of very tall grass with stiff hollow stems which are used for canes or for making furniture

ban an order to put a stop to something

banana a long fruit with a thick yellow skin

band a group of people, sometimes playing musical instruments

bandage a piece of cloth for covering up a wound

bandit a robber, usually one who robs people on the roads while they are travelling

bang a loud and sudden noise. The same word also means to hit something hard.

bangle a bracelet in the shape of a large ring

banister a rail to hold on to at the side of a staircase

banjo a musical instrument which you play by plucking the strings

bank a place where people put their money so that it will be safe

banknotes paper money

banner a flag, sometimes with two poles

banquet a feast; a special dinner party

bar a long shaped piece of hard material, usually metal or wood. The same word also means a counter where you can buy drinks.

barbecue an outdoor party where meat is cooked over an open fire

barbed wire wire twisted so that sharp points stick out. It is used as fencing.

barber a man who cuts hair and shaves beards

bare without covering or decoration

bargain something you buy that costs less than the usual price. The same word also means to argue with the seller about the price of something you want to buy.

barge a cargo boat which has a flat bottom

bark the tough covering on a tree trunk and branches. The same word also means the loud sharp noise dogs and some other animals make.

barley a plant from which we get a kind of grain; the name of that grain

barn a large farm building used mainly for storing grain, hay and other crops

baron a nobleman

barracks the buildings where soldiers live

barrel a container made of curved pieces of wood held together with hoops

barren not able to produce fruit, plants, babies or seeds. The land in deserts and on some mountains is barren because nothing will grow there.

barrier something, like a fence or wall, that stops you from going further

barrow a two-wheeled cart that is pushed by a man

base the bottom of anything; the part on which something stands or is built

basement the lowest part of a building, usually below the ground

bash to hit something so hard that it is smashed or dented

bashful another word for shy

basin a round bowl for holding water

bask to warm yourself in the sun

basket a container made of straw or thin pieces of wood. It has a handle so that you can carry things inside.

bat   a shaped piece of wood used to hit a ball in games. The same word also means a small mouse-like animal that flies at night.

bath   a large container in which you can wash yourself all over

bathe   to take a bath or a swim

bathroom   a room with a bath in it

baton   a stick for beating time to music

batter   to beat or strike something over and over again. The same word also means a mixture of flour and liquid used in cooking.

battery   a container for storing electricity

battle   a fight

battleship   a warship with heavy armour and big guns

bawl   to cry out or shout very loudly

bay   a part of the sea or lake that makes a curve into the land

bayonet   a long sharp blade attached to a rifle, so that it can be used like a spear

bazaar   a market-place or fair where things are sold, usually to raise money for charity

beach   the strip of land next to the sea, covered with sand or pebbles

beacon a signalling light, like a bonfire or lighthouse

bead a small ball with a hole through it. You can thread many beads together to make a necklace

beak the hard pointed part of a bird's mouth

beaker a tall cup, often without a handle

beam a long thick piece of wood. The same word also means a ray of light.

bean a vegetable with large seeds that grow in pods

bear a large heavy animal with thick shaggy fur and a very short tail. The same word also means to carry something or to put up with something.

beard the hair on a man's chin

bearing the part of a machine on which another part moves or slides. The same word also means the way you carry yourself.

beast an animal

beat to hit over and over again; to keep regular time in music. The same word also means to do better than another person or team in a game or a race.

beautiful lovely; very pretty

beauty great loveliness

become to grow to be something

bed a soft place to sleep, with blankets and a pillow. The same word is also used for a place where flowers are grown, and for the bottom of the sea

bedclothes   the covers on a bed

bedroom   a room where there is a bed

bedside   the space next to a bed

bedspread   the top cover on a bed

bee   an insect with four wings and a sting. It makes honey and wax.

beech   a kind of tree with smooth silver-grey bark

beef   the meat from a cow or bull

beehive   a house for bees

bee-line   a straight line between two places

beer   a strong drink made from malt

beetle   an insect with four wings. The two front wings are hard, and protect the back wings when they are folded.

beetroot   a dark red vegetable

before   ahead; in front

beg   to ask earnestly or humbly for something

beggar   someone who lives by asking for money and food from others

begin   to start

beginning   the start of something

behave   to act in a good or a bad way, showing good or bad behaviour

behaviour   how you act or behave; your manners

behind   at the back of; to the rear of

believe   to accept what someone says as the truth; to have faith

bell   a cup-shaped piece of metal which makes a ringing sound when struck

bellow   to roar or yell loudly

belly   another word for stomach

belong   to be the property of; to be part of

below   underneath; at a lower level

belt   a long strip of material, usually leather, which fastens around the waist

bench   a long seat, usually made of wood

bend   to make something crooked or curved

beneath   under something

beret   (*say berray*)   a round flat soft hat

berry   any small round juicy fruit without a stone

berth   a bed or bunk in a ship or train

beside   near; next to

best   most good

bet   to risk your money against someone else's on the result of a game or race

betray   to give away secret information; to let someone down by breaking a promise

better   more than good. The same word also means more clever or skilful than someone else.

between   in a space; among

eware to be very careful about something that may be dangerous, like a fierce dog or railway lines

ewilder to puzzle someone or make him not sure what to do

eyond farther on, or farther away

ib a cloth tied around a baby's neck, to stop food getting on his clothes

ible a holy book

icycle a two-wheeled vehicle with a saddle

id to command or invite: to make an offer

ig large; important

ill a written note of how much money is owing for work which has been done, or for something which has been bought. The same word also means a bird's beak.

illiards a game played with hard balls and long sticks called cues, on a table covered with thick green cloth

illy-goat a male goat

in a container for corn, bread, coal, or rubbish

ind to fasten or tie together

ingo a game of lucky numbers that can be played by lots of people at once, in a hall or theatre

inoculars a kind of double telescope with tubes for both eyes

birch a tree with smooth silvery or white bark

bird a winged animal covered with feathers

birdcage a small cage for a pet bird

birth coming into life, being born

birthday the day of the year when you were born

biscuit a crisp flat cake

bisect to divide in two equal parts

bit a small piece of something

bitch a female dog

bite to take a piece out of something with your teeth

bitter tasting sharp and sour; not sweet or sugary

black the darkest colour of all. Coal is black.

blackberry a small juicy black fruit which grows wild

blackbird a black songbird with a yellow beak

blackboard a wooden board painted black. You write on it with chalk.

blackcurrant a small black berry

blacksmith a man who makes and mends iron things. He also puts metal shoes on horses.

blade one leaf of grass or wheat. The same word also means the cutting part of a knife.

blame to find fault with

blanc-mange (*say blah-monj*) a milk jelly

blank   without any writing or marks, empty

blanket   a woollen bed-cover

blast   an explosion: a strong sudden gust of air

blaze   a brightly burning fire

bleach   to take the colour out of something

bleak   cold and windy: without cheer

bleat   the crying sound made by a lamb, sheep or goat

bleed   to lose blood

blend   to mix together

bless   to make holy; to ask God to show favour to someone or something

blind   not able to see

blink   to open and shut your eyes very quickly

blister   a swelling on the skin, like a small bubble, often filled with water or blood

blizzard   a very windy snow storm

block   a big piece of something, like wood, metal or stone. The same word also means to be in the way of something.

blood   the red liquid which circulates round your body

bloom   to come into flower

blossom   another name for flower, especially the flowers on fruit trees and shrubs

blot   a spot or mark, usually of ink

blouse a loose garment covering the upper part of the body. It is worn by girls and women.

blow to push air out of your mouth. The same word also means a hard knock.

blue a colour. When the sun shines the sky is blue.

bluebell a wild flower with blue blossoms shaped like bells

blue tit a prettily coloured small wild bird

blunt the opposite of sharp, having a dull edge or point

blur to make something look dim or not clear

blush to go pink in the face because you are shy, ashamed or upset by something

boar a male pig

board a long flat piece of wood

boarder someone who pays to sleep and eat in someone else's house: someone who lives at boarding school in term time

boarding school a school where children live during term time

boast to talk a lot about how good you are at things, to praise yourself or things which belong to you

boat a small ship

bob to move up and down

bobbin   a spool for holding thread or yarn

bodice   the part of a dress from the neck to the waist. It is usually close-fitting.

body   the whole of a person or animal

bodyguard   a person who guards and protects someone

bog   wet, marshy ground

boil   to make water so hot that it bubbles and makes steam. The same word also means a sore swelling on your body.

boiler   a container for boiling water, often for making steam

bold   brave; without fear

bolt   a metal fastening for doors and gates. The same word also means to run away.

bomb   a metal case that can be exploded

bomber   an aeroplane which carries bombs

bond   anything which binds or fastens something together

bone   one of the hard white parts which are joined together to make the skeletons of our bodies

bonfire   a fire out of doors, usually in a garden

bonnet   a kind of hat that ties under the chin

bonny   pretty; healthy-looking

book   pages of print bound together in a cover

bookcase   a set of shelves for books

boom   a long deep noise, like the sound the word boom makes when you say it

boomerang   a curved wooden weapon that turns in the air and comes back to the person who throws it

boot   a shoe that covers part of the leg as well as the foot

bootee   a soft woollen boot for babies

border   the outside edge of something

bore   to make a deep hole in something by twisting a tool round and round. The same word also means to make someone tired by dull talk.

born   starting to live

borrow   to take something which you intend to give back

bosom   another word for breast. The same word also means close, like a bosom friend.

boss   a chief or leader

botany   the study of plants

bother   to annoy or worry. The same word also means fuss or trouble.

bottle   a container, usually made of glass. It has a narrow neck and is used to hold liquids.

bottom   the lowest part of anything

bough   (*rhymes with now*)   the branch of a tree

boulder   a very large rock or stone

bounce   to spring up again after hitting the ground

bound to leap forward. The same word also means fastened or tied.

bouquet (*say bookay*) a bunch of flowers

bow (*rhymes with so*) a kind of knot used to tie ribbon or string. The same word also means a curved strip of wood with a string, used for shooting arrows.

bow (*rhymes with now*) a way of showing respect. You bend forward and lower your head.

bowl a deep round dish for holding liquids or food. The same word also means to throw a ball overarm, as in cricket.

box a stiff-sided container

boxer a man who fights with his fists, usually in padded gloves

boy a male child who will grow up to be a man

bracelet a pretty chain or ring you wear on your arm

braces pieces of elastic which go over the shoulders to hold trousers up

bracket a piece of metal or wood that holds a shelf up

brag another word for boast

braid to weave strips of hair or material in and out to make a plait

brain the part inside your head that sends and receives messages and thoughts and controls what your body does

brake the part of a vehicle which stops the wheels from going round

bramble a blackberry bush

bran the skin of grains, which is separated from the flour

branch the arm of a tree that grows out of its trunk

brand a mark on something to show whose it is or who made it

brass a yellowish metal made by melting copper and zinc together

brave not running away from danger, even when you are afraid

brawn strength; powerful muscle

bray the cry of a donkey

bread a food made mostly from flour, and baked into a loaf

breadth how wide or broad something is

break to pull apart; to damage or spoil something

breakfast the first meal of the day

breast the top front part of the body

breath the air that is taken in and forced out by the lungs

breathe to take air into the body and force it out again

breed to produce young ones

breeze a gentle wind

brewery a place where beer is made

brick a block of baked clay used in building

bride   a woman on her wedding day

bridesmaid   an unmarried woman who attends the
bride on her wedding day

bridge   something built over a road or river so that
you can get across to the other side

brief   short; not long

brigade   a group of men in uniform who work
together, like a brigade of soldiers or a brigade
of firemen

bright   shining; giving out light

brilliant   very bright; dazzling. The same word also
means very clever.

brim   the upper edge of something, like the brim of
a cup. The same word also means the part of a
hat that sticks out all round.

bring   to carry something with you when you come

brisk   quick; lively

bristle   a short stiff hair

brittle   easily broken

broad   wide; the opposite of narrow

broadbean   a bean with a wide pod

broadcast   to send out radio or television
programmes of news, music and entertainment

bronchitis   an illness in the throat and chest that
makes you cough a lot

bronze a reddish-brown metal made by melting copper and tin together

brooch (*say broach*) an ornament which can be pinned to clothing

brood to sit quietly and think about something rather anxiously. The same word also means young birds all hatched in one nest at the same time.

brook a small stream

broom a brush with a long handle, for cleaning floors

broth a kind of thin soup

brother a son of the same parents

brow the forehead

brown a colour. Chocolate is brown.

brownie a junior member of the Girl Guides. The same word also means a kind of goblin who is supposed to help with housework.

bruise a dark-coloured mark where the skin has been hit but not broken

brush a bunch of hairs on a handle, used for cleaning or painting or doing your hair

bubble a ball of liquid containing gas or air

bucket a container with a handle for holding or carrying water

buckle a fastening on a belt or strap

bud a flower or leaf not fully open

budge to move a little

budgerigar a bird like a very small parrot, often kept as a pet

buffalo a wild ox

buffers flat metal plates at each end of a railway carriage or engine, or at the end of a railway track. They prevent damage from bumping.

bug a tiny insect

build to make or construct

builder a man who puts up buildings

building anything with a roof and walls

bulb a small glass lamp which gives out electric light. The same word also means the rounded root from which some flowers grow.

bulge to swell out

bulk a large amount

bull the male of cattle. Male elephants are also called bulls.

bulldog a heavily-built dog with a large head and powerful shoulders

bulldozer a powerful tractor used for shifting large loads of earth, sand or rubbish

bullet a small piece of metal which is shot from a gun

bullfrog a large frog with a deep voice

bullock a young bull

bully someone who picks on others weaker or smaller than himself

bulrush a kind of tall reed that grows in or near water

bumblebee a large fluffy bee which makes a loud buzzing noise

bump a swelling, or a raised part of anything. The same word also means to knock into something.

bumper a piece of curved metal on the front and back of cars to protect them if they bump into something

bun a small soft round cake

bunch a group of things tied or growing together, like a bunch of flowers

bundle a number of articles bound together, like a bundle of clothes

bungalow a house without an upstairs

bunk a shelf-like bed attached to a wall

buoy (*say boy*) something floating on the water but anchored to the sea bed. It marks the places where there is danger, or where small boats can be tied up.

burden a load that is very heavy to carry

bureau a chest of drawers with a writing desk on top. The same word also means an office.

burglar someone who breaks into buildings at night and steals things

burial   the burying of something, like a dead body, in the ground

burn   to be on fire, or to set something on fire

burrow   a hole in the ground which has been dug by wild animals to live in. Rabbits and foxes live in burrows.

burst   to give way suddenly; to rush forward

bury   to put something somewhere deep, usually under the ground

bus   a large vehicle which carries many people

busby   a tall fur hat that some soldiers wear

bush   a shrub, like a small tree with lots of branches growing close to the ground

business (*say bizness*)   occupation, work

bust   a sculpture of someone's head, shoulders and chest. Sometimes the word means the breast.

bustle   to rush about busily

busy   having something to do all the time; working hard

butcher   a man who cuts up meat and sells it

butt   a large barrel for holding liquids

butter   a kind of soft yellow fat made from cream

buttercup   a bright yellow wildflower

butterfly   an insect with large coloured wings

butterscotch   a sweet made from sugar and butter

buttocks the two rounded parts which you sit on, at the back of your body below the waist

button a round fastening on clothes; any small knob

buttonhole a narrow hole for a button to fit into

buy to give money in exchange for something

buzz the humming sound a bee makes

cab the place in an engine or lorry where the driver sits. The same word also means a taxi.

cabbage a vegetable with green or purple leaves growing tightly together in a round ball

cabin a small house or hut made of logs or other rough materials. The same word also means a room for passengers on a ship or aeroplane.

cabinet a kind of cupboard with glass doors where you keep ornaments or collections of things

cable a very strong thick rope, sometimes made of pieces of wire twisted together

cackle the loud excited noise made by hens

cactus a plant with thick leaves and stems, often covered with prickles, which grows in hot dry countries. You can also grow small ones as house plants.

caddy a small airtight box to keep tea in

cadet a boy or young man who is learning to be an officer in the army or navy or air force

café (*say caffay*) a place where you can buy a meal or a snack; a small restaurant

cafeteria an eating-place where you fetch your own food from a counter

cage a box or room with bars, where birds or animals are kept

cake a sweet food made of flour, fat, eggs and sugar and baked in an oven. The same word also means a small flat lump of something, like a cake of soap.

calamity something awful that happens, like an earthquake or an aeroplane crash in which many people are killed or hurt

calendar a list of all the days and dates in each week and each month of a year

calf a young cow or bull. The same word also means the thick part of the back of your leg below the knee.

call to shout or cry out. The same word also means to stop at someone's house for a short time.

calm quiet; still. The same word also means not getting upset or excited when something unusual happens.

camel a big animal with a long neck and one or two humps on its back. It carries people or things from place to place in some hot countries.

camera a kind of box for taking photographs

camouflage to disguise something so that it is hidden from the enemy

camp to live outdoors in a tent. The same word also means the place where the tents are set up.

can a small airtight metal container for food or liquids. The same word also means to be able to do something.

canal a very big ditch, dug across land and filled with water so that ships and boats can move along it

canary a small yellow bird kept as a pet because of its sweet song

candle a rounded stick of wax with a wick through the middle. It burns and gives light.

candlestick a holder for a candle

cane the hard stem of a plant or small palm tree. The same word also means a light walking stick.

cannon a big heavy gun, sometimes on wheels

canoe a narrow light boat. You use a paddle to make it move through the water.

canopy a covering hung over a throne or a bed

canteen a place in a factory or office building where food and drinks are sold to the people who work there

canvas tough strong cloth used for tents and sails and for painting pictures on

cap a small soft hat, usually with a peak

capacity the greatest amount a container will hold

cape a piece of clothing without sleeves that goes over the back and shoulders and fastens round

the neck. The same word also means a point of
land sticking out into the sea.

caper to leap or jump about happily

capital a large letter of the alphabet, like A, B, C.
The same word also means the chief city in a
country.

capsule a tiny container for medicine, which melts
after you have swallowed it. The same word
also means the closed cabin of a spacecraft.

captain a person who is in charge of a group of
people, like soldiers, sailors or a football team

captive someone who has been captured and held
prisoner

capture to catch someone and hold him by force

car a motor for driving from place to place

caramel a kind of sweet, like toffee, made with
sugar and butter cooked together until the
mixture is sticky and brown

caravan a small house on wheels, pulled by a car or
a horse. The same word also means a group of
people travelling together for safety, especially
in the desert.

carburettor part of a car engine that mixes air and
petrol

card stiff paper. Sometimes it is cut into pieces
with pictures and greetings for special days like
birthdays and Christmas. Cards are also used
in playing games.

cardboard very thick stiff paper

cardigan a knitted woollen jacket

care a worry or trouble. The same word also means to look after someone who needs help.

careful giving special attention to what you are doing

careless not taking trouble or thinking about what you are doing

caretaker a person who looks after a building or part of a building

cargo a ship's load

carnation a pink, red, yellow or white flower with a spicy smell

carol a song of joy or praise, most often heard at Christmas time

carpenter a man who makes things out of wood

carpet a thick soft woven covering for the floor

carriage a vehicle for carrying passengers from place to place. The same word also means part of a railway train.

carrot a long pointed orange vegetable that grows under the ground

carry to take something from one place to another

carry-cot a bed with handles, used to carry a small baby about

cart an open wagon with only two wheels

cartoon a short funny film or drawing in a newspaper

cartridge a case for holding the gunpowder and bullet to be shot from a gun

carve to shape a piece of wood or to cut patterns on it with a knife. The same word also means to cut meat into slices.

case a kind of box to keep or carry things in

cash coins and banknotes

cashier someone who looks after the money in a bank, a shop or an office

cast to throw something with force. The same word also means to shape something by pouring hot metal or liquid plaster into a mould.

castaway a person who has been shipwrecked

castle an old building with thick stone walls to resist enemy attacks

cat a furry animal, usually kept as a pet

catalogue a list of things in a special order, like a list of books in a library

catapult a Y-shaped stick with elastic attached, used for shooting stones

catch to get hold of something

caterpillar a grub that turns into a moth or butterfly

cathedral a very large and important church

catkins small fluffy flowers without petals. They grow on willow and hazel trees.

cattle cows, bulls and oxen

cauliflower   a cabbage-like vegetable with a large white part in the middle that is good to eat

cause   to make something happen

caution   carefulness; watchfulness

cavalry   soldiers on horseback

cave   a big hole in rocks or in the side of a hill

cavern   a large cave

caw   the loud hoarse cry of a crow

cease   to stop

ceiling   the top of a room

celandine   a yellow wildflower

celebration   a party on a special day like a birthday or a national holiday

celery   a vegetable with long white stalks and pale green leaves

cell   a room where prisoners are kept. The same word also means the small bare room a monk lives in.

cellar   an underground room where coal and wine and other things are kept

cement   a greyish powdered clay mixture that hardens when it is mixed with sand and water. It is used to stick bricks and other building materials together.

cemetery a place where people who have died are buried

centigrade divided into a hundred degrees. On a centigrade thermometer freezing point is shown as zero and boiling point at 100.

centimetre a hundredth part of a metre

centre the middle part of anything

century a hundred years

cereal any kind of grain used as food

ceremony an important and special happening, like a wedding or a coronation

certain sure; without any doubt

certificate something written or printed which proves that something is true; written proof that you have passed an examination

chaffinch a small wild bird with a cheerful song

chain metal rings joined together

chair a single seat with a back to lean against

chalet (*say shalay*) a small wooden house, usually with overhanging eaves

chalk a soft white stone which can be made into sticks for writing on the blackboard

challenge to invite someone to try to beat you at something, such as running, swimming or wrestling

champion someone who is better at a sport than anyone else. The same word also means to stick up for someone or defend him.

chance something that happens without being planned. The same word also means an opportunity.

change to make something different from what it was before

channel a deep narrow strip of sea-water between two pieces of land. The same word also means a kind of path through the air used for television programmes.

chap a boy or a man

chapel a small church or a separate part of a large church

chapter a section of a book divided off by numbers — chapter 1, chapter 2

character what a person is like. Someone's character may be good or bad, honest or dishonest, nice or nasty.

charade (*say sharahd*) a game in which you act out parts of a word and then the whole word

charcoal a hard blackened piece of burnt wood. You can draw pictures with it.

charge the cost of something. The same word also means to rush at something. To be in charge is to be in control.

chariot an open two-wheeled carriage drawn by horses. In olden days chariots were used in wars and in races.

charity   a feeling of kindness and affection towards other people: a gift of money, food or shelter to people in need

charm   to make others think you are nice and pleasant to know. The same word also means something that has magic powers or can bring good luck.

chart   a map, usually of the sea

chase   to run after

chassis (*say shassee*)   the framework which forms the base of a car

chat   to talk with someone in a friendly way

chatter   to talk a lot about things that are not important

chatterbox   someone who is always talking

chauffeur (*say shofer*)   a man who is paid to drive someone else's car

cheap   not costing much money

cheat   to do something that is not honest or right, like copying someone else's answers during a test

check   to go back over something to make sure it is correct. The same word also means a pattern with squares in it.

cheek   the soft side of your face below your eyes and either side of your nose

cheeky   saucy; a bit rude

cheer   to shout at someone to do his best or to show you are pleased. The same word also means joy, happiness.

cheerful happy; joyful

cheese a food made from milk

chemist a man who makes up medicines and sells them, as well as things like toothpaste and soap

chemistry the study of what things are made of

cheque (*say check*) a special piece of paper you write on to ask your bank to pay some of your money to someone

cherry a sweet round red or yellow fruit with a stone in it

cherub a winged creature with a child's face

chess a game for two people, using pieces called chessmen on a board marked with black and white squares

chest a large strong box with a lid. The same word also means the front part of your body between your neck and your waist.

chestnut a nut. One kind is good to eat when it is roasted, and the other kind is a conker.

chew to crush or grind with your teeth

chewing gum a sweet that you keep chewing but do not swallow

chick a baby bird

chicken a young hen or cock

chicken-pox an illness. You have a high temperature and lots of spots all over you.

chief a leader or ruler. We also use the word to mean that something is the most important, like the chief city in a country.

chilblain a painful itchy swelling on your hands or feet in cold weather

child a boy or girl who is older than a baby, but who is not yet grown up

children boys and girls

chilly feeling cold

chime a musical sound made by a set of bells, usually in a clock

chimney an opening from the fireplace to the roof to let the smoke out

chimpanzee a very clever ape, smaller than a gorilla

chin the part of your face under your mouth

china cups and plates made from a kind of clay

chink a narrow crack or slit. The same word also means a clinking sound, as when you rattle coins together.

chip to knock a small piece off something like a cup or vase. The same word also means a small piece of fried potato.

chipmunk a small wild animal, like a squirrel with stripes

chirp a short shrill sound made by some birds and insects

chisel a tool with a cutting edge at the end, used for cutting stone or wood

chocolate a sweet brown food or drink made from cocoa

choir (*say kwire*) a group of people trained to sing together

choke to find it hard to breathe because there is something in your throat or because there is smoke in your lungs

choose to take one thing rather than another

chop to cut something with hard blows. The same word also means a small piece of meat on a bone.

chopper something you use to chop with, like an axe

chopsticks two thin pieces of wood or ivory used for eating food by people living in some far-eastern countries

chorus the part of a song that comes after each verse, when everyone joins in the singing. The same word means the people on a stage who dance and sing together.

christen to give a baby its first or Christian name, usually in a church

Christian a follower of Jesus Christ

Christmas the birthday of Jesus Christ

chrome a silvery-looking metal

chrysanthemum an autumn flower with lots of brightly coloured curving petals

chuck to throw

chuckle to laugh quietly

chum a close friend

church a building where people go to worship God

churn a machine for making butter: a milk can

cigar tobacco leaves rolled tightly together, for smoking

cigarette finely cut pieces of tobacco rolled in thin paper, for smoking

cinders coal or wood that has been burned but not burned away to ashes

cinema a building where films are shown

circle a completely round ring

circulate to move around and come back to the beginning. The blood in our veins circulates through every part of our bodies.

circus a travelling show with acrobats and animals and clowns who do all sorts of tricks

city a very large town

civil to do with people or the government, like the civil service, but not the armed forces. The same word means polite.

claim to demand something because you believe you should have it

clang a loud deep echoing noise, usually made by big bells

clank a deep ringing sound such as the noise made by rattling heavy chains

clap to slap the palms of your hands together

clash a loud noise when things are banged together

clasp to hold tightly. The same word also means a fastening for a brooch or other jewellery.

class a number of children or older people learning something together

classroom a room in school where children learn things

clatter a rattling noise, as when you are washing up crockery and cutlery

claw one of the sharp curved nails on the foot of an animal or bird

clay soft sticky earth that can be baked to make bricks or crockery

clean without dirt or dust

cleaner someone or something that cleans things

cleanse to make clean

clear bright, or with nothing in the way, so that you can see things easily

clench to close your teeth or fists tightly together

clerk someone who does office work, such as answering letters and keeping accounts

clever quick to learn; able to do things very well

click   a short snapping sound

cliff   a high steep rock

climate   the kind of weather a country usually has. Africa and India have hot climates.

climb   to move upwards using your feet and sometimes your hands to hold on

cling   to hold on to something tightly

clinic   a place where people go to see doctors or nurses

clink   a small ringing sound, as when you gently touch coins or glasses together

clip   to cut or trim something with scissors. The same word also means a small metal fastening for holding letters or papers together.

clipper   a large fast ship with many sails

cloak   a loose garment without sleeves, usually longer than a cape

cloakroom   a place where you can leave hats and coats: a lavatory

clock   a machine that tells you what the time is

clockwise   the direction in which clock hands move

clockwork   machinery like that which is inside a clock

clog   to block up something like a drainpipe. The same word also means a wooden shoe.

close   to shut. The same word also means very near.

cloth   a woven material that clothes and coverings are made of

clothes   all the things you wear, except jewellery

clothing   another word for clothes

cloud   millions of tiny drops of water floating close together in the sky. Clouds may look white or grey.

clout   a blow. The same word also means a piece of cloth.

clover   a wild plant with leaves in three rounded parts and small tight pink or white heads

clown   a man in a circus. He has a funny painted face and makes us laugh.

club   a group of people who meet to do things together, like playing tennis or golf. The same word also means a heavy stick.

cluck   the soft short sound a hen makes to her chicks

clue   something that helps you to find the answer to a puzzle or mystery

clump   a number of plants or trees growing close together

clumsy   not graceful; not good at handling things

cluster   a bunch; a group

clutch   to grab something and hold on to it tightly. The same word also means a part of machinery used for starting and stopping an engine.

coach   a large carriage pulled by horses, with an

outside seat in front for the driver. The same
word also means a large motor vehicle for long
journeys.

coal a hard black mineral used for fuel

coalman a man who delivers coal

coarse rough

coast the border of land next to the sea. The same
word also means to go downhill in a car
without using the engine, or on a bicycle
without pedalling.

coat an outer garment with sleeves

cobbler someone who makes or mends boots and
shoes

cobweb a very thin net made by a spider to trap
insects

cock a male bird: a rooster

cockerel a young cock

cocoa a brown powder made from cocoa beans. It
is used to make hot drinks and chocolate.

coconut a very large nut with milky liquid inside

cod a large sea fish caught for food

code secret words or signals used to send
messages

coffee a hot drink made from ground-up roasted
coffee beans

coffin   a large wooden or metal box that a dead body is put into

coil   to wind in rings

coin   a piece of money made of metal

coke   fuel made from coal when the gas has been baked out of it

cold   the opposite of hot. A fire is hot and ice is cold. The same word also means an illness which affects the nose and throat.

collapse   to fall to pieces or to fall down

collar   the part of a garment round the neck

collect   to bring together or gather together

collection   the things you collect, such as a collection of stamps, seashells or old coins

college   a place where you can go on studying after you have left secondary school

collide   to bump or run into something

collie   a large longhaired sheepdog

colliery   a coal mine

colour   Red, yellow, blue and green are colours.

colt   a young horse

column   a pillar. The same word also means a line of soldiers and a list of numbers.

comb   a short piece of plastic or metal with teeth in it, used to tidy your hair

combine   to mix or join together

combine-harvester a farm machine that does two jobs. It harvests the grain and then threshes it.

come to move near

comedian an actor who makes people laugh

comedy a funny play or film

comfortable to be feeling at ease, without pain or worry

comic a picture paper for children

command to tell someone he must do something

commence to begin

commit to do something, usually something wrong like a crime

committee a small number of people who meet together to arrange things

common ordinary; usual. The same word also means an open piece of ground that doesn't belong to one person.

commotion noise and fuss

companion someone who goes somewhere with you; a friend

company a group of people working together in a business. The same word also means a group of people who are guests at a party.

compare to say how things are alike or different; to show whether one thing is better or worse than another

compass an instrument for showing north, south, east and west

compasses a tool for drawing a circle

compel to force someone to do something

compete to be in a test or race to see who is best

competition a test of how much people know or how good they are at something. The winner usually gets a prize.

complain to tell about something that is upsetting you, or that you think is wrong

complete whole, with nothing missing

complicated not easy or simple; difficult to understand

compliment something nice said about someone to please him

composition things put together to make a whole thing. A number of notes make a musical composition, and words written down make a written composition.

comprehension the ability to understand

compress to press together

conceal to hide; to keep secret

conceited thinking too highly of yourself

concentrate to bring together in one place: to think hard about one thing

concern to do with; to interest or trouble yourself with

concert a musical entertainment

conclude to end or finish something

concrete a mixture of cement, gravel and water that dries as hard as stone

condense to make something smaller or shorter by taking part of it away. Condensed milk has some of the liquid taken out of it to make it thicker and smaller in quantity.

condition how something or someone is

conduct to guide; to lead; to be in charge. The same word also means behaviour.

conductor someone who collects bus or train tickets. The same word also means a man who stands in front of an orchestra and beats time.

cone something round at the bottom and pointed at the top, like an ice-cream cone or a clown's hat. The same word also means the fruits of pine or fir trees, which are cone-shaped.

confess to say that you have done wrong; to own up to something

confetti tiny bits of coloured paper thrown at a wedding for good luck

confuse to mix up; to mistake one thing for another

congratulate to tell a person you are glad about something good that has happened to him

congregation people gathered together in a church

conjuror someone who can do magic tricks

conker a round hard shiny brown nut in a prickly outer covering. It grows on a horse chestnut tree.

connect to join or fasten together

conquer   to win; to overcome

conscious   knowing what is going on; able to hear and understand what is happening around you

consent   to agree

conservatory   a heated greenhouse where plants can be grown

consider   to think carefully about something

considerable   rather large; much

considerate   kind to others; thoughtful about how other people feel

consonants   the sounds of a language other than vowels. They are written by all the letters of the alphabet except *a e i o u.*

constable   a policeman

construct   to build or make

contain   to hold something inside. A bottle contains milk.

container   something that holds things inside, such as a box or bottle

contented   happy; pleased with what you have

contents   what is contained in something

continual   keeping on; frequent

continue   to go on doing something, or to begin doing something again

continuous   keeping on without stopping

contract   to become smaller. The same word also means an agreement.

contradict to disagree entirely; to say that something someone has said is not true

control to guide or check something, such as a vehicle or a machine. The same word also means to be in command of other people.

convenient easy to use or reach

convent a building for nuns to live in

conversation talk between two or more people

convict someone who has been sent to prison

convince to persuade someone that you are right

cook to heat food and make it ready for eating

cooker a stove on which food is cooked

cookery the art or practice of cooking

cool not quite cold

copper a reddish-brown metal. The same word also means a copper-coloured coin.

copy to make or do something exactly the same as something else

coral a hard, stony pink or white material made from millions of piled-up skeletons of tiny sea animals, sometimes used to make jewellery

corduroy cotton cloth with ridges in it

core the middle part of something, like the part where the seeds are in an apple or pear

corgi a small dog with short legs

cork a stopper put in the top of a bottle to keep the liquid from spilling out

corn the seeds of grain plants, like wheat, barley and oats. The same word also means a hard lump of skin on your toe, that hurts when your shoe is too tight.

corner where two walls or roads meet

cornet a musical instrument like a trumpet. The same word also means an ice cream in a kind of biscuit shaped like a cone.

cornflakes a breakfast cereal eaten cold with milk and sugar

cornflower a bright blue summer flower

coronation the crowning of a king or queen

corporation a group of people who run the business of a town

correct right; true; with no mistakes

corridor a long narrow passage with rooms leading off it

cosmonaut someone who travels in space

cost what you have to pay for something

costly expensive; not cheap

costume style of clothing worn at different times in history. The same word also means clothes worn by actors on the stage.

cosy comfortable; snug and warm

cot a bed for a small child

cottage a small house in the country

cotton thread or cloth made from the cotton plant

cottonwool   the fluffy part of the cotton plant

couch   a long soft seat where more than one person can sit

cough   the loud noise you make when you choke or when you have a sore throat or bronchitis

council   a group of people who meet to talk and decide about problems to do with controlling a town or city

count   to name numbers in their proper order. The same word also means a nobleman.

countdown   the counting backwards of seconds of time before a rocket is fired

counter   a kind of long table in a shop or café

country   the land outside a town. Another country means another part of the world.

county   a part or section of a country

couple   two of anything; a pair

coupon   a printed piece of paper which can be exchanged for something else

courage   without fear even when there is danger; bravery

course   the direction in which anything goes. The same word also means a number of lessons on one special subject.

court   the place where a king or a judge does his work

courtyard   an enclosed space near or within a building

cousin   the child of your aunt or uncle

cover   to put one thing over another so as to hide it

cow   the female of cattle

coward   someone who is not brave

cowboy   a man on a ranch
who looks after cattle

cowshed   a farm building where cattle are kept

cowslip   a small yellow spring wildflower

crab   a water animal with a hard shell and
big claws

crack   a split or long thin opening in something. The
same word also means a sharp, sudden noise.

cracker   a small firework. The same word also
means a thin crisp biscuit.

crackle   a crisp sound, like the sound made by the
word when you say it. Dry twigs crackle on a
fire.

cradle   a baby's bed with rockers instead of legs

craftsman   someone who is good at making things
with his hands

crafty   artful; cunning

crane   a machine for lifting heavy things. The same
word also means a long-legged bird.

crash   a loud smashing noise

crate   a container for packing vegetables, eggs, fruit
and bottles. It is made of thin pieces of wood
fastened together.

crawl to move forward on your hands and knees. The same word means a stroke used in swimming.

crayon a soft kind of pencil that you use to colour a picture

crazy silly; mad

cream the rich fatty part of milk

creamery a place where butter and cheese are made or sold

crease a mark made by folding or doubling something like paper or cloth

create to make or bring into being

creator maker or producer

creature a living thing, such as a bird, insect or other animal

creek a small stream or part of a river

creep to move slowly and quietly, sometimes on your hands and knees

crêpe (*say crayp*) thin wrinkly cloth

crescent anything shaped like the new moon

cress a plant used in salads

crew people who work on a ship or aeroplane

crib a small bed with bars to keep a young child from falling out

cricket a game played with a bat and ball and several players. The same word means an insect something like a grasshopper, which makes a chirping sound.

crime something wrong that can be punished by law

crimson a deep red colour with some blue in it

crinkle to wrinkle something by squeezing it tightly

cripple a person who is lame or whose arms or legs have been damaged in some way

crisp hard and dry; easily broken, like a potato crisp or a piece of toast

crisscross straight lines crossing over each other

croak a deep, hoarse noise, like the sound a frog makes

crock a pot or a jar

crocodile a dangerous scaly reptile which lives in or near water in hot countries

crocus a small garden plant, with bright purple, yellow or white flowers

crook a long hooked stick or staff carried by shepherds. The same word also means someone who is not honest.

crooked not straight

crop grain, fruit or vegetables grown on the land for food. The same word also means a short whip used in hunting.

cross anything shaped like × or +. The same word also means rather angry.

crosspatch someone who is bad-tempered

crow a large black bird, with a harsh croaking voice. The same word also means the sound a cock makes.

crowd a lot of people all together in one place

crown the gold head dress worn by a king or queen

cruel very unkind

cruise a sea voyage for pleasure

crumb a very small piece of bread, cake or biscuit

crumble to break into little pieces

crumple to crush something into wrinkles

crunch to make a loud noise when you are chewing something hard and crisp like an apple or toast

crush to press together or squash something

crust the hard outer covering of something like a loaf of bread or a pie

crutch a special stick with a padded top piece that fits under the armpit. Lame people use crutches to help them to walk.

cry to weep tears. The same word also means to make a loud sound of joy or sorrow.

crystal a hard mineral that is transparent

cub the name given to some young animals such as bears and foxes

cube a shape having six sides of equal measurement, like a cube of sugar

cuckoo a bird that lays its eggs in other birds' nests. It makes a noise that sounds like its name, cuckoo.

cucumber a long green watery vegetable used in salads

cuddle to hug with affection

cue a stick used in the game of billiards

cuff the end of a sleeve at the wrist. The same word also means a blow with the palm of your hand.

cunning clever in a rather unpleasant way; crafty

cup a small bowl-shaped container with a handle, used for drinking

cupboard a set of shelves with doors

curb to stop or hold something back

curds the thick part of milk, when it is separated to make cheese. The thin watery part is called whey.

cure to help someone who is ill to get well again; to heal

curious wanting to know or find out. The same word also means odd or strange.

curl to twist hair into curves or rings

curlers rollers or pins which girls and women put into their hair to make it curly

curly not straight; going around in curves

currant a small dried grape: a red, black or white sour-tasting berry that grows on bushes

current a flow or stream of air, water or electricity. The same word also means at present, happening now.

curtain a piece of cloth hanging down to cover a window or a stage in a theatre

curtsey a bow girls and women make by bending their knees

curve a line shaped like part of a circle

cushion a soft pillow covered with pretty material. It is used to rest against on a chair or settee.

custard milk, eggs and sugar cooked together to make a pudding or sauce

custom what is usually done; habit

customer someone who wants to buy something, usually in a shop

cut to make pieces of something smaller by using scissors or a knife

cutlery what you eat food with — knives, forks and spoons

cycle another word for bicycle

cyclone a very bad storm in which a strong wind goes round and round in a circle

cylinder a hollow rounded piece of metal often used in machinery

cymbals two metal musical instruments, shaped like plates

dab to touch something lightly

daffodil a yellow spring flower shaped rather like a trumpet

daft foolish or silly

dagger a short sword

dahlia a garden plant with brightly coloured flowers

daily every day

dainty pretty; delicate

dairy a place where milk, butter and cheese are kept

daisy a small field flower with white or pink petals around a yellow centre

dale low ground between hills; a small valley

dam a special kind of wall which checks a flow of water

damage harm or injury

damp slightly wet

dance to move in time to music

dandelion a wild plant with bright yellow flowers

dandy a man who spends a lot of time on his clothes and the way he looks

danger risk; the opposite of safety

dangerous not safe

dare to have the courage to do something

daring full of courage; plucky

dark without light. When the sun goes down, the sky grows dark.

darling someone dearly loved. We may call a person or animal we love, darling.

darn   to mend a hole by sewing it over with wool or cotton

dart   a kind of small arrow thrown by hand

dartboard   the target at which you aim in the game of darts

dash   to rush suddenly. The same word also means a short straight line in writing, like this —.

date   a time when something happens; a certain hour, day, month or year. The same word also means a sweet sticky fruit with a stone.

daughter   a female child of a father and a mother

dawdle   to waste time

dawn   the first light of day

day   the time between sunrise and sunset

dazed   being confused or bewildered

dazzle   to blind someone for a short time by suddenly shining a strong bright light into his eyes

dead   without life

deaf   not able to hear

deal   an amount. The same word also means to do business with.

dear   much loved, precious. The same word also means highly priced.

death   the end of life

debt   what someone owes to someone else

decay   to become rotten or to fall into ruins

deceive   to make someone believe something that is not true; to cheat

decent   proper; acceptable to most people

decide   to make up your mind; to settle something

decimal   numbered by tens

deck   the flooring on a boat or ship

deck chair   a folding chair used for resting out of doors

declare   to say something clearly; to make something known

decorate   to make something look pretty. We decorate a Christmas tree.

deed   an act; something done

deep   a long way down

deer   a wild animal with four long legs. The male has large branched horns.

defeat   to beat someone at a game; to conquer

defend   to try to keep yourself from being beaten; to guard someone or something against attack

definite   certain; without doubt

defy   to refuse to obey

degree   a unit of measurement. Temperature is measured in degrees centigrade or fahrenheit.

delay   to put off to a later time

deliberate   not by accident; done on purpose

delicate   easily broken or damaged; fragile

delicatessen   a shop that sells food ready to eat, such as cooked meats or special cheeses and salads

delicious   very good to taste and eat

delight   great pleasure or joy

deliver   to hand something over to someone else. The same word also means to rescue or set free.

dell   a little valley in a wood or forest

demand   to ask for something in a commanding way, without saying please

demon   an evil spirit or devil

den   a cave or shelter where some kinds of wild animals live

dense   closely-packed; thick; difficult to make your way through, like a dense forest

dent   a bent place in something, usually caused by a blow

dentist   someone who takes care of your teeth

deny   to say that something someone says is not true

depart   to go away or leave a place

department   a part or section of a shop, office or factory

depend   to count on someone; to rely

deposit   to put something down and leave it. The same word also means a small amount of money left in part payment for something.

depot (*say depo*)   a storehouse

depth   how deep something is

descend   to go down

describe   to say what something or someone is like

desert   land on which very little can grow because there is no water. Deserts are often made of sand.

deserve   to earn something, like deserving a reward for working hard

design   to draw a pattern; to make a plan or drawing

desire   to want something very much. The same word also means a wish or request.

desk   a table used for reading or writing

despair   to give up hope

despise   to dislike something or someone very much because you think they are no good and worthless

dessert   the fruit or pudding served after the main part of a meal

destroy   to kill or ruin completely

destroyer a warship that guards a fleet of ships against attack

detail a small part

determine to settle or decide; to make up your mind to do something

detest to hate very much

develop to grow gradually, as a puppy develops into a dog, or a bud develops into a flower

devil an evil spirit. The word is often used to describe a wicked or cruel person.

dew drops of moisture which cover the ground in the very early morning

diagonal a line drawn from one corner of something to the opposite corner

diagram a plan or drawing to show what a thing is, or how it works

dial the flat round part of something with numbers on it, like a clock, a watch or a telephone

dialect a special way of speaking a language in one part of a country

diameter a straight line drawn from one side of a circle to the other, passing through the centre

diamond a very hard colourless precious stone which sparkles

diary a book in which you write down what you do from day to day

dice a pair of small cubes with different numbers of spots on each side. They are used in games like ludo and snakes and ladders.

dictionary   a book which tells you the meanings of words and how to spell them

die   to stop living or to come to an end. The same word also means one of a pair of dice.

diesel engine   an engine that burns a special kind of oil

differ   to be unlike; to disagree

difference   what makes something not like something else

different   not the same

difficult   hard to do or to understand

dig   to make a hole in the ground

dignified   acting in a serious manner

dim   not bright

dimple   a little hollow, usually in your cheek or chin

din   loud noise, usually going on for a long time

dine   to eat dinner

dingy   dull and dirty looking

dinner   the main meal of the day

dinosaur   a very large reptile that lived millions and millions of years ago

dip   to go in and out of something quickly. You dip your spoon into a bowl of soup.

dire   dreadful; terrible

direct   straight; the quickest or shortest way. The same word also means to show someone the way.

direction   the way something goes, such as a road going north, south, east or west

dirt   mud, soil, or earth

dirty   not clean; in need of washing

disagree   to have a different opinion about something

disappear   to go away very quickly; to vanish

disappoint   to find that things are not as you had hoped they would be. When you do not win a game you may be disappointed.

disaster   a calamity; a great misfortune

disc   anything which is round and flat, such as a gramophone record

disciple   a follower or pupil

discourage   to make someone feel that what he is doing is not worth while so that he will stop trying

discover   to find out; to see something for the first time

discovery   something which has been found out

discuss   to talk about

discussion   an argument or talk with other people

disease   illness; sickness

disgrace   shame

disguise   to change your appearance by wearing different clothes, a wig or a false moustache, so that people do not recognize you

disgust   a feeling of dislike so strong that it makes you feel sick

dish   a plate for food

dishonest   the opposite of honest

dislike   the opposite of like

dismay   fear; a feeling of being upset and sad

dismiss   to send someone away or tell him they can leave

distance   the length of space between two places

distant   far away. A far-off place is distant.

distemper   an illness which young dogs get. The same word also means a kind of paint used on walls in rooms.

distinct   separate; clearly seen or heard

distress   a feeling of great pain, sorrow or worry

district   a part of a town or county

disturb   to interrupt or cause trouble

disturbance   a noisy interruption, as when people upset a meeting by shouting out

ditch   a very long narrow trench which is dug in the ground to drain water away

divan   a couch

dive to plunge headfirst into water or down through the air

diver someone who goes down into very deep water

divide to separate into parts

dizzy feeling that your head is spinning round and round; giddy

do to perform or make

dock a place where ships are unloaded or repaired

doctor someone who helps you to get better when you are ill

dodge to jump quickly to one side so as not to bump into something

dog a four-legged animal which is often kept as a pet

doll a toy made to look like a person

dome a curved roof like half a ball

domino a small oblong piece of wood either painted black with white dots or white with black dots. You play a game with dominoes.

donkey an animal like a small horse with long ears

doodle to draw or scribble while thinking about or doing something else

door a kind of barrier which has to be opened to go in or out of a building or room. It is usually made of wood and fitted with a handle.

doorstep the step just outside a doorway

doorway the frame into which a door is fitted

dormitory   a big room with lots of beds

dormouse   a kind of mouse with a furry tail, rather like a squirrel

dose   the exact amount of medicine you should take at one time

dot   a small round mark

double   twice as much

double-decker   a bus with an upstairs

doubtful   not being sure, not quite believing

dough   a thick floury mixture which is baked into bread or cakes

dove   a pretty bird, rather like a pigeon

doze   to close your eyes because you are sleepy, but not quite asleep

dozen   twelve of anything

drag   to pull something heavily along the ground

dragon   an imaginary animal which breathes fire. You read about dragons in fairy stories.

dragonfly   a large flying insect with transparent wings

drain   to take away water or some other liquid

drake   a male duck

draught a gust of cold air. The same word also means a small wooden disc used in the game of draughts.

draw to make a picture with pencils or crayons. The same word also means to pull.

drawbridge a bridge that can be let down or drawn up

drawer a kind of box that fits into a piece of furniture. It slides in and out.

drawing pin a pin with a large flat head

dread great fear

dreadful causing great fear; terrible; awful

dream the thoughts that go on in your mind after you are asleep

drench to soak right through

dress to put on clothes. The same word also means a garment worn by girls and women.

dressing-gown a garment which you wear over your nightdress or pyjamas

dressing table a table with a mirror where you can sit to do your hair

dressmaker a person who makes clothes for women, girls and small children

dribble to let food or liquid trickle out of the mouth on to the chin. The same word also means to run with a football at your feet.

drift to be floated or blown along

drill to bore a hole in something with a special tool. The same word also means regular practice.

drink   to swallow water, milk, or some other liquid

drip   to drop in little drops. A tap drips when only a little water comes out very slowly.

drive   to make something move along

driver   someone who drives

drizzle   light rain

droop   to bend or flop over

drop   to let something fall. The same word also means a tiny bead of water.

drown   to die under water because there is no air to breathe

drowsy   feeling very sleepy

drum   a hollow instrument that you beat to make music

drumstick   the stick you use to beat a drum. The same word also means the leg of a chicken or turkey.

dry   not wet; without water

duck   a rather large web-footed bird which swims. The same word also means to dip underwater for a moment; to lower your head; to dodge something.

due   owing; not paid

duke   a nobleman of high rank

dull uninteresting, not lively or sharp, with no sparkle

dumb not able to speak

dummy a model made to look like a person: something in place of the real thing

dump to throw down or get rid of something

dumpling a lump of flour and fat cooked in a stew

dunce a fool; someone who is slow to learn things

dungeon a dark prison cell, usually under the ground

during throughout: while something is happening

dusk the part of the evening just before the sky gets really dark

dust tiny bits of powdery dirt

dustbin a container for dirt and rubbish

duster a cloth used for wiping away dust

dustman a man who empties dustbins

dustpan a container into which you sweep dust

duty what you ought to do or have to do

dwarf an animal, plant, or person who is much smaller than most others of the same kind

dye colouring powder or liquid used to change the colour of cloth or other material

dynamite a powerful exploding substance

eager wanting very much to do something; keen

eagle a large bird of prey, with a sharp curved beak and claws

ear the part of the body you hear with. The same word means a spike of grain such as an ear of corn or barley.

earl a nobleman of high rank

early in good time; near the beginning

earn to get something, usually money, in return for working: to deserve

earnest serious; sincere

earring jewellery which is worn on the ear

earth the planet we live on; the world. The same word also means the ground in a garden or field.

earthquake a violent shaking of the earth's surface

ease freedom from pain or worry: rest from work

easel a special stand on which a painter can put his picture while he is working on it

easily with no difficulty

east the direction in which the sun rises; the opposite direction to west

Easter the time when Christians believe Jesus came back from the dead

easy not difficult; not hard to do or understand

eat to chew and swallow food

eaves the edges of the roof sticking out over the top of the walls

ebb the going back of the sea from the shore when the tide goes out

echo a sound that comes back to you, as when you shout in a tunnel or cave

eclipse a cutting off of light from the sun when the moon comes between the sun and the earth

edge the cutting side of a knife. The same word also means the end of something like a table or a shelf.

educate to help someone to learn

education helping people to learn, usually in schools or colleges

eel a very long fish that looks like a snake

effect the result caused by something, as when the effect of cold weather is to make you shiver

effort a hard try. When you use all your strength you are making an effort.

egg an oval object with a thin shell. A chicken, like other baby birds, lives inside an egg before it is born.

eiderdown a quilt, usually filled with feathers from an eider duck

elastic material made with rubber which stretches easily

elbow the joint in the middle of your arm

elder older. The same word also means a large shrub with clusters of white blossoms which turn into purple berries later.

elderberry   a purple berry from which wine can be
  made

electricity   an invisible force which is used to make
  light and heat. It also makes power for engines
  and machinery.

elephant   a very large animal with a long nose called
  a trunk

elf   a tiny mischievous fairy

elsewhere   not here; somewhere else; in another
  place

embarrass   to make someone feel shy by teasing or
  by making difficulties for them

embroider   to make pretty designs on material using
  a needle and thread

emerald   a bright green precious stone

emperor   the male ruler of an empire

empire   a group of countries or states which is ruled
  by one king or queen, called an emperor or
  empress

employ   to give work to someone, usually for
  payment

empress   an emperor's wife, or the female ruler of
  an empire

empty   with nothing or no one inside

enamel   a hard shiny paint used on such things as
  bathtubs, cookers and saucepans

enclose   to put something in an envelope or package: to surround or shut in by a fence or wall

encourage   to help someone to keep on trying; to try to give courage to someone

encyclopaedia   a book or set of books which tells you something about every subject

end   the last part; the finish

endure   to bear trouble or pain with courage and patience

enemy   someone who fights against you or your country

engage   to hire someone to work for you

engaged   bound by a promise, as when a man and a woman are engaged to be married to each other

engine   a machine which makes things work. Aeroplanes, cars and trains are all moved by engines.

engineer   someone who makes or looks after machines. The same word also means someone who plans and builds dams, roads, railways and bridges.

enjoy   to take pleasure in something

enormous   very large; huge

enough   as much as is needed and no more

enquire   to ask. The word is also spelled inquire.

enter   to go or come into a place

entertain   to amuse. The same word also means to have someone as your guest.

entertainment   a show or concert that entertains or amuses you

enthusiasm   keenness; eagerness; great interest in something

entire   complete; whole

entrance   a doorway or way into a place

entry   the act of entering

envelope   a folded piece of paper in which you put letters for posting

envy   a wish to have something that belongs to someone else

episode   an event in a story: a complete short story which is part of a longer story

equal   of the same size, quantity or value as something else

equator   an imaginary line around the middle of the earth's surface

equipment   all the things needed to do a job, play a game, or go on an expedition

erect   upright; standing up straight

errand   a short journey to take a message or to deliver or collect something

error   a mistake; something that has been done incorrectly

escalator   a moving staircase

escape   to get free, usually from something unpleasant

especially   most of all; of greatest importance

estimate to guess the size, quantity or value of something

eve evening. The same word also means the day before a special event, like Christmas Eve.

even level; smooth. The same word also means any number that can be divided exactly by two.

evening the time between afternoon and night

event something that happens

ever always; for all time

evergreen a shrub or tree that keeps its leaves and stays green all the year round

every each one

everybody each person

everyday daily. The same word also means usual or common.

everyone another word for everybody

everything all things

everywhere in all places

evil very bad; wicked; the opposite of good

ewe a female sheep

exactly just right; correctly; with no mistakes

exaggerate to say that something is bigger or more important than it really is

examination a number of questions that you have to answer, usually in writing, to show how much you know about something; another word for test

examine   to look at closely and carefully

example   a sample; a single one of many. The same word also means a pattern to be copied, as when you follow somebody's good example.

excellent   very, very good

except   leaving out; apart from

exchange   to give one thing in return for another

exciting   Something which makes you feel strongly is exciting. You can feel excited if something nice is going to happen.

exclaim   to speak or call out suddenly

excuse   a reason for not doing something. It may be a good excuse or a poor excuse.

exercise   the training of your mind or body

exhaust   to use up or tire out completely. The same word also means the pipe which lets out the gases from a motor engine.

exhibition   a public show of things such as works of art, flowers, or furniture

exist   to be: to continue to live

exit   the way out of a place

expand   to grow bigger; to swell

expect   to look forward to; to think something will happen

expedition   a journey to explore a place or to search for something, such as rare plants and animals

expense   cost; payment of money

expensive costing a lot of money; dear

experience knowledge of something because you have seen or done it

experiment something tried out to see what will happen: a test to find out something

expert someone who knows a lot about a particular subject

explain to give the meaning of something; to make something clear

explanation anything said or written that helps you to understand clearly the reason for something

explode to burst or blow up with a loud bang

explore to travel to places to try to find out all about them

explosion the act of blowing up or exploding: a sudden burst with a loud noise

express to put thoughts into words, music or pictures. The same word also means a fast train.

expression the look on faces when people are happy, sad, or worried. The same word also means a way of saying things.

extend to stretch out; to make longer

extent the length, size or area of anything

extra more than necessary or expected

extraordinary very unusual; not ordinary; surprising

eye one of the two parts of your face that you see with

eyebrow a little line of hairs over each eye

eyelash one of the little hairs that grow along the edge of the eyelid

eyepiece the glass part of a telescope or microscope which you look through

fable a short story, usually about animals, which is meant to teach us a lesson

face the front of your head

fact a thing that everyone knows is true and not imaginary

factory a building where things are made in large quantities, usually by machine

fade to lose colour or freshness

faggot a bundle of sticks

fahrenheit a measurement of heat having the freezing point of water marked at 32 degrees and the boiling point at 212 degrees

fail not to be able to do something you try to do; to be unsuccessful

failing a fault or a bad habit

faint pale or weak. The same word also means feeling weak and dizzy.

fair a place with roundabouts where you have fun. The same word also means light in colour (as in fair hair) and right or good (as in fair play).

fairly not bad; reasonably good

fairy a very small person who can do magic. You read about fairies in stories for young children.

faith what you believe in: trust that what is said is true

faithful keeping your promises; believing

fake something that looks valuable but is not; a cheap copy of something

fall to drop through the air

false wrong; not keeping your promises; not faithful; not real or true

falter to stumble; to hesitate when speaking

familiar well known or close to you

family a mother and father and their children

famine great scarcity of food; starvation

famished starving

famous well known

fan something which makes a cool breeze. The same word also means someone who is very fond of a certain sport, hobby or famous person.

fancy decorated. The same word also means imagination.

fang a long pointed tooth

far a long way away

fare the price you pay for travelling on a public vehicle such as a bus

farewell an old-fashioned word for goodbye

farm a place where a farmer keeps animals and grows food

farmer   a man who looks after a farm

farmyard   ground surrounded by barns, cowsheds and other farm buildings

farther   at a greater distance away; more distant

fascinating   very attractive; very charming

fast   very quick

fasten   to join together

fastening   something that fastens or closes things tightly

fat   big and round. The same word also means the whitish greasy part of meat and bacon. Other kinds of fat are found in fish and in nuts.

fatal   causing death; disastrous

father   a man who has children in his family

fault   a mistake; anything which spoils something which is otherwise good

favour   an act of kindness which is done for someone

favourite   a person or thing which is liked better than any other

fawn   a young deer

fear   a feeling of alarm when you think you are in danger

fearful   afraid. The same word also means terrible or awful.

fearless without fear; brave

feast a large special meal with lots of good things to eat and drink

feat an act of great skill or strength

feather part of the wing or the soft coat of a bird

feeble very weak; not strong

feed to give food to someone or some animal

feel to find out what something is like by touching it

feet more than one foot

fellow a man: a companion

felt a thick woollen material used for hats

female people and animals who can become mothers. Girls and women are of the female sex but boys and men are of the male sex.

feminine like, or to do with, women or girls

fence something put round a field or garden to keep animals and people in or out

fender a metal guard in front of a fire

fern a plant which has lacy, feathery leaves but no flowers

ferret a small animal used for hunting out rabbits and rats

ferry   a boat used to take people or cars across water where there is no bridge

fertile   able to produce seeds or plants abundantly

fester   to rot; to become infected

festival   a joyful celebration with dancing, music and often feasting

fetch   to go and get

fête (*rhymes with gate*)   an outdoor entertainment or party, usually to raise money

fever   an illness which makes your body very hot and makes you feel weak and thirsty

few   not many

fib   a small lie; something which is not quite true

fiction   a made-up story or book about people and happenings that are not really true

fiddle   a violin. The same word also means to play about with something in a careless sort of way.

fiddler   a man who plays a fiddle

fidget   to move about in a restless way

field   an open piece of land, often surrounded by hedges

fierce   angry; wild

fiery   like fire; flaming or burning

fig   a soft sweet fruit which grows on a fig tree

fight   to struggle against someone or something

figure the shape of something, such as a person's body. The same word also means a number.

file a metal tool with a rough surface, used to make things smooth. The same word also means a line of people following one behind the other.

fill to put so much in a container that you cannot get any more in

film a moving picture. The same word also means a strip of material used in a camera.

filter a special strainer used to separate dirt and other solids from liquid

filthy very dirty

fin one of the wing-like parts of a fish which help it to balance and swim

final the very last; coming at the end

finally at last; at the end

find to see something you are looking for; to discover

fine excellent; very good. The same word also means sunny and dry.

finger a part of your hand. You have five fingers on each hand.

fingerprint the pattern made when you press your finger or thumb on the surface of something

finish to get to the end; to complete

fir a kind of evergreen tree with leaves like needles

fire the flames, light and heat made by something burning

fire engine   a big motor vehicle that carries the firemen and their equipment to put out a fire.

fireman   a man who helps to put out fires

fireplace   the open place under the chimney where a fire burns

fireside   the space next to a fireplace where you can sit and warm yourself

fireworks   Fireworks are usually made of gunpowder in a cardboard tube. They are set alight after dark on special days.

firm   solid; strong and not easily moved

first   at the very beginning

fish   a swimming animal which cannot live out of water. It has fins and breathes through its gills.

fisherman   a man who catches fish

fishing   the sport or business of catching fish

fishing-net   a net used for catching fish

fishing-rod   a long thin stick with a string and hook attached for catching fish

fist   a tightly closed hand

fit   to be the right size and shape for something. The same word also means in good health.

fix   to mend something. The same word also means to tie or fasten something firmly.

fizz   to bubble and make a hissing sound

flag   a piece of cloth with a coloured pattern. Each country in the world has its own flag with its own pattern.

flake a very small thin piece of something, such as a snowflake

flame the bright fire that leaps from something burning

flan an open piece of cooked pastry which is filled with custard, fruit, or some other filling

flannel a soft warm woolly material

flap to move up and down, as a bird flaps its wings. The same word also means anything which hangs loose or is hinged, such as a table flap.

flare to burst into bright light, as when a piece of wood suddenly bursts into flame

flash a sudden bright light that appears only for a moment, like a flash of lightning

flask a kind of bottle, usually made of metal or glass, for holding liquids

flat smooth; without bumps and being the same height all over. The same word also means a home on one floor which is part of a larger building.

flatten to make something flat

flavour what makes foods taste differently from each other. Ice cream comes in lots of flavours, like strawberry, vanilla and chocolate.

flax a plant from which strong threads can be obtained. The cloth woven from these threads is called linen.

flea a tiny jumping insect

flee to run away, usually because of danger

fleece the coat of wool on a sheep

fleet   a number of ships or vehicles that belong together

flesh   the soft parts of your body

flex   a wire for electricity, covered with plastic or some other material

flick   to hit something very lightly

flicker   to burn brightly and then dimly so that the light is not steady

flight   the act of flying through the air

flimsy   not strong or thick, easily broken

fling   to throw something away from you

flint   a very hard kind of stone which gives off sparks when you strike it with steel

flit   to move about very lightly and quickly

float   to rest on top of a liquid or on air. A boat floats on water, and a bubble floats on air.

flock   a large group of birds or of some animals

flood   a great overflowing of water, usually over dry land

floor   the part of a room you walk on

flop   to let yourself fall down heavily

flour   a white powder made from grain. It is used to make bread and cakes.

flow   to move along smoothly, like water

flower   the pretty coloured part of a plant

flower-pot   a pot in which you plant flowers

'flu   a shortening of the word influenza, which is an illness causing a fever and a sore throat

fluff   a light soft stuff that comes off woollen cloth and similar materials, such as blankets and carpets

fluid   something that can flow, such as liquid or gas

fluke   something lucky that happens by chance

flute   a long thin musical instrument which you blow into

flutter   to flap about; to move the wings quickly

fly   to move through the air. The same word also means a flying insect.

flying fish   a fish with large fins that help it to move through the air when it leaps out of the water

foal   a young horse

foam   a lot of tiny white bubbles, usually on the top of liquid or soapy water; froth

focus   to get a clear picture

foe   an enemy

fog   thick cloudy air

fold   to double something over

foliage   the leaves on trees and plants

folk   people

follow   to come after someone or something

folly silliness; a foolish action

fond loving; liking very much

font a stone basin in a church, which contains the water for christening a baby

food the things we eat to keep us alive

fool a silly person

foolish silly; stupid; not wise

foot the part of the body you stand on. The same word also means a measure of 12 inches.

football a team game in which you kick a ball and try to score goals

footpath a path or part of the road where people can walk but vehicles are not allowed

footprint the mark someone's foot leaves in wet sand or soft earth

footstep the sound a foot makes when walking

forbid to command or order someone not to do something

force power; strength

ford a place in a river where the water is shallow enough for you to walk or drive through it safely

forearm the part of your arm between your wrist and elbow

forecast to say that something will happen before it does

forehead the part of your face above your eyes

foreign   of another country: strange

forest   a large area of land where lots of trees are growing close together

forethought   a thought or plan for the future

forfeit   something you have to give up because of something you have done

forge   a blacksmith's workshop, with a furnace for heating the metal. The same word also means to copy someone else's handwriting for a dishonest purpose.

forgery   something written or painted which is not genuine: someone else's handwriting copied for a dishonest purpose

forget   not to remember

forget-me-not   a little blue flower

forgive   to pardon, to stop being cross with someone who has done something wrong

fork   a tool used to pick up food

form   shape. The same word also means a class in school, or a paper asking questions which are to be answered.

fort   a strong building made to keep enemies out

forth   onwards; out

fortnight   fourteen days; two weeks

fortress   another word for fort

fortunate   lucky

fortune   what comes by luck or chance: great riches or wealth

forward   towards the front

fossil   the remains of an animal or plant that has turned to stone after being buried for many millions of years

foul   dirty; horrible

foundations   the solid part of a building below ground level

fountain   water pushed up into the air continuously in one or more jets

fowl   a bird, usually a hen

fox   a wild animal which has a long bushy tail

fraction   a part of a whole, such as one-half ($\frac{1}{2}$) or one-third ($\frac{1}{3}$)

fragile   delicate; easily broken or damaged

fragment   a bit or piece broken off something

frame   the wood or metal around something, like a window or a picture

framework   the outline or main parts of something that the rest is built on to

fraud   dishonesty; a cheating trick

fray   a fight or quarrel

freak   a person, plant or animal whose appearance is not ordinary or normal, such as a white blackbird

freckle   a small brown spot on the skin

free   not a prisoner; able to do or say what you like. The same word also means without payment.

freeze   to become hard because of the cold, as when water turns into ice

frequent   happening often

fresh   new: healthy: not tired

fret   to be discontented; to worry

friend   someone you know well and like a lot

friendly   kind; showing friendship

frieze   a picture or pattern around the top of a wall

fright   sudden fear; alarm

frightened   afraid of something

frightful   terrible; awful

frill   an edging of lace or light material on clothing or curtains

fringe   hair cut straight across the forehead. The same word also means an edging of loose threads, usually on clothing, lampshades and rugs.

frisky   lively; playful

fritter   to waste something a little at a time. The same word also means a piece of meat or fruit fried in batter.

frizzy   very tightly curled

frock   a dress

frog   a small animal which lives in or near water and can jump a long way

frolic   to have fun; to dance and play games

front   the opposite to back; the most forward part of anything

frost   a thin icy covering on the ground when it is cold

froth   a lot of tiny white bubbles, usually on top of liquid; foam

frown   to wrinkle your forehead when you are angry or not pleased

frozen   solid with ice

fruit   a part of a bush or tree which can be eaten

fruitful   producing much fruit

fry   to cook something in fat or oil

frying pan   a round shallow pan for frying

fuel   anything used to make heat, such as coal, gas or wood

full   no room for any more

fully   completely; entirely

fun   to have fun is to have a good time and enjoy yourself

funeral   the ceremony of burying a dead person

funnel   a kind of chimney on a ship. The same word also means a tube that is wide at the top so that you can pour liquid into something without spilling it.

funny   amusing; laughable. Anything that makes you laugh is funny.

fur the soft hair on animals

furnace a place where great heat is produced by fire. Steel is made in a furnace.

furniture the things you use in a house, such as chairs, tables and beds

furrow a long narrow cut made in the ground by a plough

further more distant

fury very great anger

fuse a piece of string or material attached to something that will explode. It burns slowly to give you time to get to safety before the explosion. The same word also means a piece of wire used for safety in an electric system.

fuss a bother or worry, usually about something unimportant: unnecessary noise and bustle

future the time to come: the days, months and years ahead of us

fuzzy covered with tiny hairs or fluff. The same word also means not clear or easily seen.

gabble to speak so quickly that people find it hard to understand what you are saying

gadget a small cleverly designed tool or piece of apparatus

gain to earn or win: to add to what you already have

gale a strong wind

galleon a large sailing ship which was used by the Spaniards hundreds of years ago

gallery   the upper floor of seats in a theatre or church. The same word also means a room or building where works of art are on show.

gallon   a measure of liquid, equal to 4 quarts or 8 pints

gallop   the fastest speed at which a horse can move

galoshes   a special kind of waterproof overshoes. Sometimes the word is spelled goloshes.

gamble   to play a game for money

gambol   to skip and jump happily

game   a way of playing which has rules

gaming   another word for gambling

gander   a male goose

gang   a group of people working together. The same word also means a band of robbers or thieves.

gangster   a member of a gang of robbers and thieves

gangway   a narrow passage between rows of seats: a movable bridge between ship and shore

gantry   a bridge built over railway lines to carry signals: a support for a crane

gaol (*say jail*)   another word for prison. The word is also spelled jail.

gap   an opening or break in something

garage   a place where motor cars are kept or repaired

garden   a piece of land where flowers, fruit or vegetables are grown

garland a circle of leaves or flowers worn on the head or around the neck or hung on something as a decoration

garment any article of clothing

garter a ring made of elastic which keeps a stocking from falling down

gas something like air, neither solid nor liquid, which can fill space. It is usually invisible. Gas that burns comes through pipes and is used for cooking and heating.

gash a long deep cut or wound

gasp to take a quick deep breath: to struggle for breath

gate a door in a fence, wall or hedge

gather to collect; to pick up one by one

gay happy and lively

gaze to look at something steadily; to stare

gear things that belong to you, such as clothes or tools. The same word also means the working part of a car or bicycle which changes the speed.

geese more than one goose

gem any precious stone; a jewel

general a commander in the army. The same word also means usual; happening everywhere.

generous   kind in sharing or giving things to others

gentle   quiet; soft or soothing

gentleman   a kind and honourable man

genuine   real; true; not a fake or copy

geography   the study of the surface of the earth and the people and animals living there

geometry   the part of mathematics to do with lines, angles and figures such as triangles and circles

geranium   a plant, usually with scarlet, white or bright pink flowers

germ   a very tiny bit of animal or plant life that you can only see under a microscope. Some germs cause diseases.

get   to receive; to fetch. The same word also means to become, as when we say someone will get well, or get rich.

ghost   the spirit of a dead person

giant   a very big strong person, usually in fairy stories

giddy   having a feeling that things are going round and round

gift   something which is given as a present

gigantic   enormous; giant-like

giggle   to laugh in a silly way

gill   an opening for breathing in a fish's skin

ginger   the root of a plant. It tastes spicy and makes your mouth feel hot.

gingerbread   a cake or biscuit which is made with ginger

gipsy   someone who belongs to a race of dark people who originally came from India. Gipsies wander from place to place and usually have no permanent home. The word is sometimes spelled gypsy.

giraffe   a tall animal with a very long neck

girder   a long heavy piece of metal or wood used to strengthen buildings, bridges and parts of railways

girl   a female child; a child who will grow up to be a woman

give   to hand something over freely to someone else

glacier   a mass of ice that moves very slowly down a mountainside

glad   pleased; happy

glance   a quick look

glare   a dazzling bright light. The same word also means to stare angrily at someone.

glass   a hard material you can see through. Windows are made of glass.

glasses   two framed pieces of a special kind of glass. If you cannot see well, glasses help you to see better.

gleam   to shine, but not brightly. Old metal gleams when it is polished.

glen a narrow valley

glide to move smoothly and easily; to flow gently

glider a light aeroplane which can fly for some time without an engine after being launched

glimmer to shine faintly and unsteadily

glimpse a very brief sight of someone or something

glint to gleam or glimmer

glisten to shine or gleam

glitter to sparkle; to reflect light brightly

globe a round object, like a ball or the world

gloomy dark; dim: miserable; the opposite of cheerful

glove a covering for the hand. It fits around each finger.

glow to burn without flames; to give out a steady light

glue a strong paste which sticks things together

glum silent and sad; gloomy

glutton a person who is greedy and eats too much

gnarled twisted and lumpy, like the trunk of a very old tree

gnash to grind your teeth together when you are very angry

gnat a small flying insect which stings

gnaw to wear something away by scraping at it with teeth, as when a dog gnaws at a bone

gnome a dwarf you read about in stories

go to start off or move

goal a kind of target. In football you have to kick the ball into the goal which is the space between two posts.

goat an animal rather like a sheep. It usually has horns and a little beard.

gobble to swallow food quickly without chewing it

goblet a kind of drinking cup with no handle

goblin a mischievous elf or fairy

God the Creator of everything

gold a yellow shiny metal which is worth a lot of money

golden the colour of gold; made of gold

goldfish a small fish often kept as a pet. It is usually a pretty reddish-gold colour.

golf a game which is played with a small white ball and a set of long-handled clubs

goloshes another way of spelling galoshes

gong a round metal disc which makes a deep ringing sound when you hit it

good right or satisfactory; kind; nice

goodbye a word said to someone who is just going away

goodness   the act of being good or kind

goods   things bought and sold

goose   a big bird, like a duck with a long neck

gooseberry   the fruit of the gooseberry bush. It is usually green with a rather hairy skin.

gorgeous   splendid; magnificent; richly coloured and beautiful

gorilla   the largest kind of ape. It lives in Africa.

gorse   a prickly shrub with bright yellow flowers

gosling   a young goose

gossip   chatter about other people, sometimes spiteful and unkind

govern   to rule or control

government   a group of people who have the power to make laws and decide what is best for the country

gown   a woman's dress. The same word also means a long loose-fitting robe or cloak.

grab   to seize hold of something suddenly

graceful   easy and smooth in movement; the opposite of clumsy

gracious   kind; charming

grade a way of deciding how good something is. If one kind of apple is better than another, it will be graded higher.

gradual happening slowly, a bit at a time

grain the seeds of some plants that are used as food. The same word also means a very small piece of something hard, like a grain of sand.

grammar the study of the way people put words together when they speak or write

gramme a very small weight, the thousandth part of a kilogramme

gramophone an instrument on which you can play records of music or words; another word for record-player

grand important; large; splendid

grandfather the father of your mother or father

grandmother the mother of your mother or father

granite a very hard rock used for buildings and for kerbstones

grant to give, to allow as a favour

grape green, purple or red fruit that grows in bunches on a vine

grapefruit a round fruit like a large orange with a yellow skin and a sharp taste

graph a diagram, usually on squared paper, that shows how a series of measurements changes

grasp to seize and hold tightly

grass a low green plant which has many thin leaves and covers fields and lawns

grasshopper   a hopping, leaping insect. It makes a chirping noise by rubbing its wings or legs together.

grass-snake   a small and harmless snake

grate   a framework of iron for holding a fire in a fireplace. The same word also means to rub something, such as a piece of cheese, against a rough surface to reduce it to small particles.

grateful   giving thanks, thankful

grave   very serious. The same word also means a hole in the ground where a dead person is buried.

gravel   lots of little pebbles which can be used to make paths

gravy   the juices of cooked meat, sometimes mixed with flour to make it thicker

graze   to eat grass. The same word also means to scrape the skin.

grease   a thick oily substance; softened animal fat

great   large; big. The same word also means important or famous.

greed   a great longing to have more of something, even though you already have enough

green   the colour of grass in springtime

greengrocer   a man who sells vegetables and fruit

greenhouse   a glass house where plants are grown

greet   to welcome; to speak to someone when you meet

greeting a welcome: a kind wish often written on a birthday or Christmas card

grey the colour of the sky when there is no sun

greyhound a very thin dog with long legs, used for racing

grief great sadness

grieve to be very sad about something; to be very unhappy

grim stern, unsmiling, and often cruel

grime dirt that sticks on and is hard to get off

grin to smile broadly

grind to crush something into a powder. The same word also means to rub together, like grinding your teeth.

grip to hold on to something tightly

grit a small piece of dirt or sand. The same word also means to grind.

groan a deep unhappy sound of pain or sorrow

grocer a man who sells many kinds of food and household supplies

groove a long narrow cut hollowed out, usually in wood or metal

grope to feel for something with your hands because you cannot see well

gross very fat or big. The same word also means 12 dozen (144).

ground the earth we walk on

groundsheet a waterproof sheet which you lie on when you camp

group a number of people or things together in one place

grouse a bird that lives on the moors. The same word also means to grumble.

grove a small wood, a few trees

grow to get bigger

growl to make a low rumbling noise deep down in the throat. Dogs and lions growl when they are angry or afraid.

grown-up fully grown, adult·

grub a soft fat new-born insect

grudge a feeling of unfriendliness or dislike for someone

gruff rough in manner; stern

grumble to find fault and say you are not satisfied

grumpy bad-tempered

grunt to make a noise like a pig

guard to look after someone or something and see that nothing harms it, or is harmed by it

guardian someone who guards or looks after someone or something

guess to answer a question without knowing for sure that it is the right answer

guest a visitor; someone you invite to your house, or to a restaurant

guidance explaining or showing the way to someone

guide someone who shows people the way. He leads and helps them.

guilt a feeling of having done something wrong

guinea one pound and one shilling or one pound and five new pence

guinea-pig a small furry animal with short ears and tail, often kept as a pet

guitar a musical instrument. It has strings which you pluck to make music.

gulf a very large bay that cuts into the land: a very deep hollow in the earth

gull a web-footed sea bird, usually coloured grey and white

gullet a part inside your body which is like a tube. It leads from your mouth to your stomach.

gulp to take a quick deep swallow of food or air

gum sticky stuff which you use to fasten things together. The same word also means a soft sweet which you chew but don't swallow.

gun a machine which shoots bullets

gunpowder a special powder which explodes when you set light to it

gurgle to make a bubbly sound, as when water is let out of a bath

gush to rush out suddenly, as when water rushes out of a burst pipe

gust a sudden burst or rushing out of wind or laughter

gutter a narrow hollow for draining off rain water, usually on a roof or at the roadside

gymnasium a large room fitted with ropes, bars and all kinds of equipment for exercise

gypsy another way of spelling gipsy

habit something you do regularly and often, almost without thinking about it, such as brushing your teeth

haddock a sea fish, rather like a cod

hail frozen rain which falls as little lumps of ice

hair the soft covering which grows on your head

hairbrush a special brush you use for tidying and arranging your hair

hairdresser someone who cuts and arranges people's hair

half one of two equal parts. When you cut something in half, you divide it into two parts which are exactly the same size.

hall the space inside the entrance of a building. The same word also means a large room used for special occasions, like a town hall.

halo a ring of light around the sun or moon, or around the heads of holy people in paintings

halt to stop

halve to divide into two equal parts

hammer a heavy tool for hitting or breaking things

hammock a swinging bed of netting or canvas hung up by ropes at each end

hamper a large basket with a lid, often used for carrying food. The same word also means to hinder.

hamster a little furry animal, usually golden-brown in colour. It is often kept as a pet.

hand the end of your arm which you use to hold things

handbag a small light bag that you can carry in your hand

handful as much as your hand will hold; a small number or quantity

handicap to make something more difficult for someone

handicraft work in which things are made by hand and not by machine

handkerchief a small piece of cloth for wiping your nose or eyes

handle the part of something by which you can hold it, like the handle of a cup. The same word also means to touch or hold things with your hands.

handlebar the part of a bicycle you hold on to and steer with

handsome good-looking

handwork work, like sewing or clay modelling, which you do with your hands

handy useful and clever with your hands. The same word also means near; close at hand.

hang to fasten something to a firm support so that it swings freely, but cannot fall

hangar a large shed for aircraft

hanger a shaped piece of metal or wood to hang clothes on so that they don't get wrinkled

haphazard not planned; happening by chance

happen to take place

happiness joy; gladness

happy full of joy

harbour a sheltered place where ships stay before going out to sea

hard not soft. Stones are hard. The same word also means difficult.

harden to make or become hard

hardly scarcely; only just

hardy tough; brave

hare an animal like a large rabbit

harm to damage or hurt

harmful doing harm or damage

harmless the opposite of harmful; doing no harm

harness the straps and other equipment worn by a horse

harp a big musical instrument shaped like a triangle. It has strings which you pluck to make music.

harpoon a sharp spear attached to a rope, used for hunting whales

harsh rough or unkind

harvest the gathering of grain and fruit

haste hurry

hasten to hurry up

hat a covering for the head

hatch to break out of the eggshell, as when baby birds and chicks are hatched

hatchet a small axe

hate to dislike someone or something very much

haughty full of pride

haul to drag along; to pull

haunt to visit a place very often

haunted lived in or visited by ghosts

have to own or to hold

havoc very great damage, as when trees are blown down in a strong wind

hawk a bird of prey that hunts small birds and animals

hawthorn a kind of large bush which grows wild. It has pink or white flowers in spring and red berries in the autumn.

hay dried grass used for feeding animals

haze mist or thin cloud

hazel a small nut tree

head the part of your body above your neck. The same word also means a person who is in charge; a chief or leader.

head dress something very decorative worn on the head on special occasions or as part of a costume

headmaster a man who is responsible for all the teachers and pupils in a school

headmistress a woman who is responsible for all the teachers and pupils in a school

heal to make someone well again

health how your body feels. You have good health when you are not ill.

healthy well in body and mind; free from illness

heap a pile, like a heap of dead leaves

hear to use your ears to listen to sounds

heart the part of your body which pumps the blood around inside you

hearth the floor of a fireplace

heat to make something hot

heater something that produces heat, such as an electric fire

heath   an open area where nothing much grows except small shrubs; a moor

heathen   a person who does not believe in God. Sometimes heathens worship idols.

heather   a small wild plant which has white or purple flowers. It often grows on moors and heaths.

heave   to haul or lift something up with a great effort

heaven   the home of God. The same word also sometimes means the sky.

heavy   difficult to pick up and carry away; weighing a lot

hedge   lots of bushes growing close together in a line, like a fence

hedgehog   a little animal with a coat like sharp needles mixed with hair

heel   the back of your foot. The same word also means the back part of your shoe.

height   how tall or high something is

heir   a man or boy who will receive money, property, or a title when the present owner dies

heiress   a woman or girl who will receive money, property, or a title when the present owner dies

helicopter   a kind of aircraft without wings which can go straight up or down in the air as well as along

hell a place of misery

helmet a covering, usually made of metal, which protects the head. Soldiers, racing-drivers, and motorbike riders wear them.

help to make something easier for a person to do. You help your mother to wash the dishes.

helpful being of help

helpless not able to help yourself or others, often because of weakness

helter-skelter a slide where you go round and round as you go down

hem an edge of cloth which is folded over and sewn to make it neat

hen a mother bird

herb a plant which is used for flavouring food or for medicine

herd a group of animals kept together, such as a herd of cows

here in this place

hero a man or boy who does something brave. The same word also means the most important man in a book or play.

heroine a girl or woman who does something brave. The same word also means the most important woman in a book or play.

heroism great bravery

herring a small seafish

herself she and no one else

hesitate   to pause because you are not sure what to do or to say next

hibernate   to sleep all through the winter, as some animals do

hiccup   to make a sharp noise in your throat, usually when you have eaten or drunk too quickly. Sometimes the word is spelled hiccough.

hide   to go where no one can see you or to put something where no one can see it. The same word also means the skin of an animal.

hide-and-seek   a game where one person hides and another tries to find him

hideous   very ugly; horrible

hiding   a beating or whipping

high   a long way up. Mountains are high.

highway   a public road

highwayman   a robber on horseback who held up travellers on the road in olden days

hill   part of the ground that is higher than the rest, but lower than a mountain

himself   he and no one else

hinder   to delay or prevent someone from doing something

hinge   a joint, usually of metal. Doors are fitted with hinges so that they can be opened and shut.

hint   to suggest something without actually saying it in so many words. You might say to someone that it is getting late as a hint that you wish he would go home.

hip one of the sides of your body just below your waist

hippopotamus a very big animal which lives in hot countries

hire to pay for the use of something for a certain length of time. You can hire a taxi. The same word also means to employ.

hiss to make a noise that sounds like s-s-s-s-s. Snakes and geese make hissing sounds.

history the study of what has happened in the world in the past

hit to knock something. The same word also sometimes means a show or a tune which is a big success.

hive a house for bees

hoard a store or stock of something hidden away. Squirrels have a hoard of nuts hidden away for the winter.

hoarse having a rough-sounding voice, as when you have a sore throat

hob a place near the hearth where things can be kept hot

hobble to walk with difficulty because you are lame

hobby something you very much like to do in your spare time, such as collecting stamps or making models

hockey a team game where you try to hit a ball into the goal with a long stick curved at one end.

Sometimes the game is played on ice, with a rubber disc instead of a ball.

hoe a long-handled garden tool for clearing weeds and loosening the earth

hold to have in your hand or your arms; to contain. The same word also means the part of a ship where cargo is kept.

hole an opening in or through something

holiday a time when you do not have to work or go to school

hollow having a space or a hole inside: a valley

holly a tree with evergreen prickly leaves and bright red berries. It is often used for decoration at Christmas.

hollyhock a tall plant with many large flowers on each stalk

holster a leather case on a belt for holding a gun

holy anything specially belonging to, or to do with God

home the place where you live

homework work done at home, usually school work

honest truthful; not likely to steal from others

honey a sweet food which is made by bees

honk the loud cry of a wild goose: the noise of a motor horn

honour to show respect for someone or something

hood a loose cloth covering for the head. It is sometimes fastened to a coat or jacket.

hoof the hard part of a horse's foot. Cattle, deer and some other animals also have hooves.

hook a curved pointed piece of metal for catching, holding, or pulling things

hooligan a rough noisy person who goes about the streets bullying people and damaging property

hoop a large ring made of metal or wood

hoot to shout scornfully at someone. The same word also means the cry of an owl at night; the sound of a motor horn.

hooter a whistle blown by steam; a siren

hop to jump on one leg or move in short jumps

hope to wish that something may happen, although you know it may not

hopeful hoping; full of hope

hopeless without hope; impossible

horde a crowd or mass of people

horizon the place where the sky and earth appear to meet

horn one of the hard sharp bony parts that grow out of the heads of some animals such as cows and goats. The same word also means a musical instrument that you blow.

horrible dreadful; ugly and awful

horrid nasty; very unpleasant

horror   a very great fear or loathing

horse   an animal used for riding
and for pulling carts,
coaches and carriages

horseback   on the back of a horse

horse chestnut   a kind of chestnut tree that conkers
grow on. It has cone-shaped bunches of white
or pink flowers in spring.

horseshoe   a curved iron shoe which is nailed to the
bottom of a horse's hoof

hose   a long thin tube used for carrying water from
a tap. The same word also means socks or
stockings.

hospital   a place where people who are ill or hurt
are looked after by doctors and nurses

host   a boy or man who has other people as his
guests: an old fashioned word for innkeeper.
The same word sometimes means a crowd or a
large number.

hostess   a girl or woman who has other people as
her guests

hot   very warm

hotel   a building with many rooms, where you pay
for a bedroom and food when you are travelling

hound   a hunting dog

hour   60 minutes

house   a building to live in

houseboat   a large flat-bottomed boat used as a
floating house

household all the people who live in the same house

hover to float or stay in one place in the air

hovercraft a vehicle without wheels that can glide very quickly over the earth's surface, both land and water

how in what way

howl to make a long loud whining noise

hub the middle of a wheel

huddle crowded closely together, sometimes to keep warm

hug to hold someone or something close to you in your arms

huge enormous; very big

hull the main part of a ship

hum to make a musical sound in your nose as though you are saying m-m-m-m without opening your mouth

human a man, woman or child. The same word also means having to do with people, not with other animals or plants.

humble the opposite of proud or boasting, meek

humorist someone who makes you laugh at his jokes and sayings

humorous funny; amusing

humour fun; jokes

hump   a lump or large bump, often on the back of an animal, like a camel's hump

hunger   a need for food

hungry   feeling you want something to eat

hunt   to chase after something which you want to catch

hunter   someone who hunts wild animals or birds for food or sport

hurdle   a kind of wooden fence which animals or people have to jump over in some races

hurl   to throw something away from you with all your strength

hurricane   a very great windstorm

hurry   to move fast in order to get somewhere more quickly, or to finish what you are doing sooner

hurt   to give pain

hurtle   to rush or dash with great force and speed

husband   a married man

husbandman   a farmer

hush   to become quiet or silent

hustle   to hurry; to make someone hurry along by pushing and shoving

hut   a small wooden house

hutch   a little wooden house for a pet rabbit

hyacinth   a spring flower which has spikes of bright, sweet-smelling blossoms

hyena   a wild animal rather like a dog. It makes a high laughing sound and lives in some hot countries.

hymn   a song which praises God

ice   water which has been frozen hard by the cold

ice cream   a frozen food made with milk and sugar

icicle   a long thin spike of ice, usually hanging from a roof

icing   a sugar coating for cakes

idea   a plan which you think of, or a picture in your mind

ideal   perfect; exactly right

idiot   a person whose mind does not work properly; a crazy person

idle   lazy; not working; doing nothing

idol   an image or statue of a person or animal that is worshipped as a god

igloo   a hut made of blocks of hard snow. It has a domed roof.

ignorant   without knowledge; not knowing

ignore   to take no notice; to pretend someone or something is not there

ill   not well; not healthy

illuminate   to light or throw light upon

illustration   a picture, usually in a book. The same

word also means an example that helps to explain something.

image an exact likeness or copy of something; a statue

imaginary something you think of that is not real

imagine to picture in your mind what something or someone is like

imitate to copy, to do something the same as someone else

immediately at once

immense enormous; very big

imp a little devil: a naughty child

important of great interest or value. The same word also means powerful.

impossible not able to be done

impress to make something stick in someone's mind

impression an idea or thought that is fixed firmly in your mind. The same word also means a mark that is made by pressing or printing.

impressive making a deep impression on the mind

improve to make better; to become better

impudent cheeky; not respectful

inch a measure of length. There are 12 inches in one foot.

incident something that happens; an event

include to count something in; to contain

increase   to get bigger or more in number

index   a list in alphabetical order, usually at the end of a book. It shows the numbers of the pages where things are mentioned in the book.

indignant   annoyed or angry about something you think is wrong

indigo   a purplish-blue colour; a dye of that colour

indoors   inside a building; the opposite of outdoors

industry   hard work. The same word also means making things in factories.

infant   a baby; a young child

infirmary   another name for a hospital

inflammable   easily set on fire

inform   to tell or give information

information   facts told to someone or given in a book; knowledge

infuriate   to make very angry

inhabit   to live in or occupy

initial   the first letter of a word or name

injection   a prick, usually in the arm with a hollow needle. Through the needle a liquid medicine is pushed into your bloodstream to make you better, or to stop you from getting an illness.

injure   to harm or hurt

injury   a hurt or wound

ink   a coloured liquid used with a pen for writing

inn a small hotel where travellers can stay, and where they can buy food and drink

innocent without guilt

inquire to ask. This word can also be spelled enquire.

inquiry a question; a seeking of information. This word can also be spelled enquiry.

inquisitive eager to find out about something; curious; nosey

insect a very small animal with six legs. Ants, bees and beetles are insects.

inside within; not outside

insist to demand; to say or ask over and over again

inspect to look carefully at something; to examine

inspector someone who examines things to make sure everything is all right. The same word also means a policeman who is in charge of other policemen.

instalment one of the parts of a serial story or film: one part of the money owed for something you pay for bit by bit

instantly at once; without delay

instead in place of

instinct an ability to do things without being taught. Baby ducks are able to swim by instinct.

instruct to teach or inform someone

instrument a tool. The same word also means something which makes music.

insult   to say something rude or hurtful

intelligent   brainy; clever at learning

intend   to mean to do something, as when you intend to pay someone back

intense   very great

interest   a wish to know more about something

interesting   attracting or holding your interest

interfere   to meddle; to hinder; to try to stop something from going on

interrupt   to break in on something which is happening, like starting to speak when someone is already speaking

interval   a period of time between two events, such as a ten-minute interval between two acts in a play

interview   a talk with someone, often broadcast or reported in a newspaper

introduce   to tell people each other's names when they meet for the first time. The same word also means to bring a new idea into what you are talking about or doing.

invade   to go into a place by force, as when an army invades the enemy's country in wartime

invalid   a person who is ill

invent   to think up, or make something which is completely new and has never been thought of or made before

invisible   not able to be seen

invite to ask someone to come to your home or to go somewhere with you

iris the coloured part of the eye. The same word also means a garden plant with large flowers and sword-shaped leaves.

iron a strong grey metal. The same word also means a tool that takes the wrinkles out of clothes.

irritate to annoy or make angry. The same word also means to itch.

island a piece of land with water all around it

isle another word for island

issue a result; a problem. The same word also means to send or give something out.

italics a kind of lettering that slants to the right, *as these words do*

itch a tickling feeling on your skin which makes you want to scratch

ivy an evergreen climbing plant

jab to poke or stab at something suddenly

jackal a wild animal that looks like a dog

jackdaw a black bird, like a small crow

jacket a short coat. The same word means a loose paper cover on a book.

jagged having sharp and rough edges

jaguar   a fierce wild animal, rather like a leopard

jail   another word for prison. Sometimes the word is spelled gaol.

jam   fruit cooked together with sugar until it is thick and soft

jar   a pottery or glass container with a wide opening

jaw   one of the two large bones your teeth grow in

jazz   a kind of lively dance music

jealous   wishing you had something someone else has; full of envy

jeans   trousers made of a strong cotton cloth

jeep   a small open motor vehicle used by the army

jeer   to make fun of someone in an unkind way

jelly   a transparent wobbly food, usually fruit-flavoured

jerk   a short sudden movement

jersey   a tight-fitting knitted pullover with sleeves

jest   to say something to make people laugh; to joke

jet   a rush of liquid or gas through a small opening in a pipe or hose. The same word also means a kind of aeroplane without propellers.

jetty   a small pier

jewel   a valuable stone, like a diamond or emerald

jewellery necklaces, bracelets, rings, brooches and other ornaments made of jewels and precious metals, such as gold and silver

jib to refuse to do something. The same word also means the small triangular sail at the front of a sailboat.

jig a jolly dance

jigsaw a fine saw that can cut wood or cardboard into small curved and straight pieces

jigsaw puzzle a puzzle made of odd-shaped pieces cut by a jigsaw. You have to put them together to make a picture.

jingle a clinking tinkling sound made by coins or bells

job work done, usually for money

jockey a boy or man who rides a horse in a race

jog to move along more quickly than walking, but not so fast as running. The same word also means to give a little push, as when you jog someone's elbow.

join to put together or fasten. The same word also means to become a member of a group, such as a club or a choir.

joiner a carpenter who makes furniture and other woodwork

joint the place where two parts of something grow or are joined together

joke something a person says or does to make you laugh

jolly cheerful; full of fun

jolt to move forward in jerky movements. The same word also means a bump or shaking-up.

jostle to push or knock against someone, usually in a crowd

journal another word for a magazine or newspaper. The same word also means a diary.

journey a trip. When you travel from one place to another you make a journey.

jovial cheerful; jolly

joy a feeling of great happiness

judge the person in authority in a court of law who decides how someone who has done wrong should be punished

jug a container with a handle, used for pouring milk and other liquids

juggler someone who is very clever at balancing things and keeping them moving in the air

juice liquid in oranges, lemons, tomatoes and other fruit and vegetables

juke-box an instrument that plays records when you put money in it

jumble a mixture of odd things

jump to spring up off the ground

jumper a loose-fitting knitted pullover with sleeves, worn mostly by girls and women

junction a place where railway lines or roads meet

jungle a forest in hot countries where plants and

trees grow so thickly that it is hard to find your way through

junior   someone who is younger or less important than others

junk   something of no use or value; rubbish. The same word also means a Chinese sailing ship.

jut   to stick out

kaleidoscope   a toy shaped like a tube, with small pieces of coloured glass which change patterns when you turn the tube round

kangaroo   an animal which can jump a long way. It has a pocket for its babies.

keel   a heavy piece of wood or metal that goes along the bottom of a boat or ship from one end to the other

keen   very interested in something. The same word also means sharp; cutting.

keep   to hold on to something and not give it away. The same word also means the strongest, inside part of a castle.

keeper   someone who looks after or guards something, like a gamekeeper or a keeper at the zoo

kennel   a small house or shelter for a dog

kerb   the edge of a pavement

kernel   the inside part of a nut that can usually be eaten

kettle   a metal container used for boiling water. It has a lid, a handle and a spout.

key   a small piece of metal, specially shaped so that it will open a lock. The same word also means a lever on a piano or typewriter.

keyboard   the keys of a piano, organ or typewriter, arranged in order

keyhole   a hole specially shaped so you can put a key in it

kick   to hit something or someone with your foot

kid   a young goat. The same word also means a child.

kidnap   to take someone away by force

kill   to cause someone or something to die

kilogramme   a unit of weight, equal to 1,000 grammes

kilometre   a unit of length, equal to 1,000 metres

kilt   a short pleated skirt with a tartan pattern

kimono   a loose garment, usually fastened with a sash

kind   friendly; good to other people. The same word also means sort or type.

kindergarten   a school or class for very young children

king   a man who rules a country usually because his family did so before him

kingdom a country ruled by a king or queen

kiosk a small open-fronted hut where you can buy
sweets, newspapers and tobacco. The same
word also means a public telephone box.

kipper a herring that has been salted and then dried
in a special kind of smoke

kiss to touch with your lips someone you like

kit all the gear needed; a complete outfit

kitchen a room where cooking is done

kite a toy made of paper or cloth on light wood. It
can be flown on the end of a string when it is
windy. The same word means a bird of prey.

kitten a young cat

knapsack a bag for food and clothes that you carry
on your back

knave a man who is not honest

knee the joint in the middle of your leg

kneel to get down on your knees

knickers short underpants worn by girls and women

knife a thin sharp piece of metal with a handle,
used for cutting

knight a nobleman. In the old days, he used to
dress in armour and fight for his king.

knit to weave wool into clothing with long needles

knob a round handle, like a door knob

knock to hit something hard or to bump into
something

knocker a thick piece of metal fastened to a door by a hinge. When you lift it and then let it drop, it makes a loud noise.

knot the place where two pieces of string or ribbon have been tied together

know to understand and be sure about something you have read or seen

knowledge what you have learned and understand about things

knuckle a finger joint

label a small piece of paper or cardboard with writing or printing on it. You stick labels on such things as jars, boxes or luggage, so that you know what is inside.

laboratory a room or building where scientific tests are carried out

labour hard work

lace a string used to fasten shoes. The same word also means material with a pretty pattern of holes.

lack to be in need of something you haven't got. If you are hungry, you lack food.

lad a boy

ladder a set of wooden or metal rungs between two long pieces of wood or metal, used for climbing up or down

ladle a spoon shaped like a small cup with a long straight handle, used for serving soup or other liquids

lady another word for a woman

ladybird   a tiny flying beetle, usually red with black spots

lag   to follow along slowly behind others

lair   a wild beast's den

lake   a very large pool of water with land all around it

lamb   a young sheep

lame   not able to walk easily because you have hurt your leg or your foot

lamp   a light, usually in a glass container, like an electric light bulb

lance   a long spear. The same word also means to cut open a boil so that the fluid can drain away.

land   the parts of the earth that are not covered by water. The same word also means to come down from the air on to land or water.

landing   coming back to land from the sea or air. The same word also means the floor at the top of the stairs.

landlady   a woman who owns a house or flat where other people pay to live

landlord   a man who owns a house or flat where other people pay to live

lane   a little road, usually in the country

language   human speech or writing. The same word also means the speech used in different countries, such as the English language and the French language.

lantern a metal and glass container for a candle or oil light. You can carry it about.

lap the top part of your legs when you are sitting down. The same word also means once around a racetrack.

larch a tree which has cones and long thin leaves like needles

lard fat from pigs, used in cooking

larder a room or cupboard where food is kept

large very big

lark a small songbird. The same word also means a frolic.

lash to hit someone with a whip: to tie up firmly

lass a girl

lasso a long rope with a sliding loop at the end. It is used to catch wild horses and cattle.

last coming at the end; after all others

latch a wood or metal fastening for a door or gate

late behind time; not early

lathe a machine for cutting and shaping pieces of wood and metal while they are being turned round

lather a foam made by using soap and water together

laugh to make a noise to show you feel happy or think something is funny

launch to start something on its way, such as launching a ship into the water, or a rocket into the air. The same word also means a large open motorboat.

laundry a place where dirty clothes are washed

lavatory a place where there is a washbasin or a water-closet (W.C.), sometimes both together

lavender a plant with lavender or purple flowers that are dried and used to make linen and clothing smell sweet

law rules made by the government of a country

lawn a smooth flat area of grass which is cut and looked after carefully

lawnmower a machine that is used to cut the grass on a lawn

lay to put something down

layer a flat covering or thickness. You put jam and cream between two layers of sponge cake.

lazy not wanting to work or make any effort

lead (*rhymes with seed*) to be first, before everyone else

lead (*rhymes with bed*) a heavy soft grey metal

leader someone who is in front or at the head of a group of people

leaf the flat, green part of a plant or tree

leak the accidental escape of liquid or gas from a hole or crack in a pipe or container

lean thin; without fat. The same word also means to rest against something, so that you are not standing up straight.

leap to jump high in the air

leap year a year with 366 days, having 29 days in February. It comes every four years.

learn to find out about things or how to do something

least the smallest in size or importance

leather the skin of animals, used to make things like shoes and gloves

leave to go away from somewhere. The same word also means to let something stay where it is.

lecture a talk given to an audience or a class at school

ledge a narrow shelf

leek a vegetable with long green leaves and a thick white stem, tasting something like an onion

leer to smile at someone in a nasty way

left the opposite side to right. You have a right hand and a left hand.

leg the part of your body which joins on to your foot. You have two legs. The same word also means one of the pieces of wood that hold up a table or chair.

legend a story from long ago which may or may not be true

leggings a covering of cloth or leather for your legs in cold weather

legion a large group of soldiers: a large number

lemon a sour yellow fruit

lemonade a drink made from lemon juice and sugar

lend to let someone have something of yours which he will give back to you

length how long something is

lengthen to make longer

lens a curved piece of glass used in eye glasses or in instruments such as telescopes and cameras

leopard a dangerous wild animal that looks like a large cat with spots

lesson something to be learned

let to agree that someone may do something; to give permission

letter how a sound looks when it is written down. Our alphabet has 26 letters. The same word also means a written message that is put in an envelope.

lettuce a garden plant with large green leaves which you can eat without cooking

level another word for flat; with no bumps

lever a bar pushed down at one end so that it lifts something on the other end

liar someone who tells lies

liberty freedom to do as you think is right

library   a room or building full of books

licence   a special piece of printed paper that you must have before you can do certain things. You need a licence to own a gun, to drive a car, or to have a television set.

lick   to touch something with your tongue, like a lollipop or an ice cream

lid   the top which can be taken off something, such as a box or saucepan

lie   to say something that you know is not true. The same word also means to rest flat.

life   the time between your birth and your death

lifeboat   a special boat kept ready to rescue people who have been shipwrecked

lift   to move or raise something up. The same word also means a large metal box or cage that carries people up and down in a tall building.

light   not heavy. The same word also means something which shines brightly so that you can see in the dark.

lighten   to make less heavy or less dark

lighter   something used to produce fire, like a cigarette lighter or a firelighter

lighthouse   a tower with a strong light to guide ships at sea in the dark

lightly   gently; not heavily

lightning   a sudden bright flash of light in the sky when there is a thunderstorm

likable   pleasant; easy to get on with. Sometimes the word is spelled likeable.

like to be fond of or be pleased with. The same word also means the same or almost the same.

likely probable; expected to happen

likeness something that looks the same as the real thing

lilac a large garden bush with sweet-smelling white or purple flowers in the spring

lily a tall garden plant with large white or brightly-coloured flowers

limb an arm or leg: a branch

lime white powder made from limestone, used for making cement. The same word also means a green-coloured sour fruit, something like a small lemon.

limit the place where something ends

limp without stiffness, like wilted flowers. The same word also means to walk in a lame way.

line a thin mark like this _____ _____

linen cloth made from the flax plant. The same word also means sheets, pillowcases, towels and other household linen.

liner a large ship that carries people and cargoes long distances

linger to hang about; to delay leaving

link one of the rings in a chain

linoleum   a stiff shiny floor covering, usually called lino for short

lint   soft woolly material used to protect sores or wounds

lion   a strong and dangerous wild animal, like a very big cat

lioness   a female lion

lips   the soft edges of the mouth

lipstick   a kind of crayon in a case, used by girls and women to colour their lips red or pink

liquid   anything which is wet and flows like water

liquorice   black chewy sweets made from sugar mixed with the root of a plant

list   words placed underneath each other in a column, like a shopping list or a list of names

listen   to try to hear something

literature   poems, stories and books

litre   a measurement of capacity

litter   rubbish or waste paper left lying about. The same word also means all the babies born to a mother animal at one time.

little   not big; small

live (*rhymes with give*)   to have life; to be alive

live (*rhymes with five*)   living; not dead; alive

lively   jolly; active; full of life

liver   an inside part of the body

living-room a room with comfortable furniture where the family gathers together to talk, read, watch television or entertain visitors

lizard a scaly reptile with four legs

llama a large animal with a long woolly coat, something like a camel without any humps

load all that can be carried at one time, like a load of bricks or a load of bananas. The same word also means to put bullets into a gun, ready for shooting.

loaf a large piece of bread with crust all over it

loan something you lend to someone for a while

loathe to hate or despise greatly

lob a stroke in tennis or cricket, when the ball goes high in the air

lobby the entrance hall in a large building

lobster a shellfish with two large strong claws

local nearby; near or close by a certain place

lock a strong fastening for a door or gate that can only be opened with a key

locomotive a railway engine

locust an insect something like a large grasshopper, that destroys crops

lodge a small house at the entrance to a park or at the gates of a large house in the country

lodger   someone who pays to live in someone else's house

loft   space under the roof which can be used as a store room

log   a thick round piece of wood. The same word also means a ship's diary.

loiter   to linger; to dawdle

loll   to sit or lie about in a lazy way

lollipop   a large sweet on the end of a stick

lone   the only one

lonely   feeling sad because you are alone

long   a big distance from one end to the other

look   to watch or try to see

looking-glass   another word for mirror

loom   a machine for weaving thread into cloth

loop   a ring of wire, string or ribbon

loose   the opposite of tight; not properly fastened

loosen   to make something less tight

lord   an important nobleman

lorry   an open motor vehicle used to carry heavy loads from place to place

lose   not to be able to find something

lot   a large number; a great many

lotion   a soothing liquid medicine that you put on sore places on your skin

lotus a waterlily that grows in some hot countries

loud noisy; easily heard

loudspeaker an instrument that makes sounds louder, so that you can hear them from a distance

lounge a room with comfortable chairs in a club, hotel or house. The same word also means to loll or lie about in a lazy way.

lovable worth lóving

love to be very fond of, to like someone or something very much

lovely beautiful or pretty; nice

low not high or tall

loyal faithful; true to someone

luck something that happens by chance. You can have good luck or bad luck.

lucky having good luck

luggage the cases, trunks or bags you take your clothes in when you travel

lukewarm in between warm and cool

lumber timber. The same word also means something big and heavy that you can't use any more, like a broken armchair or an old cooker.

lump a piece of something, usually without any special shape, like a lump of clay or dough

lunar having to do with the moon

lunch the meal eaten at midday. The word is short for luncheon.

lunge to make a sudden thrust or rush at something

lupin a large garden plant with long spikes of brightly-coloured blossoms

lurch to jerk forward on to one side

lurk to hide yourself while you are waiting about for someone or something

luscious delicious

luxury something expensive and pleasant that you would like to have but don't really need: great comfort

macaroni long stiff tubes of dried wheat paste that become soft when cooked in boiling water. You can buy it in tins, already cooked.

mace a long stick with a metal ornament on the top. It was once used as a weapon, but nowadays it is carried in processions in front of the mayor and other important people.

machine an instrument, usually made of metal, which does a job of work, like a sewing machine or a washing machine

machinery the working parts of machines; another name for machines

mackintosh a raincoat. It is often called mac for short.

mad crazy; not right in the head. Someone who is mad does not think properly, because his mind is ill. The same word also means angry.

magazine a thin book which comes out every week or month. It has different stories and pictures in it each time.

maggot   a tiny worm or grub that is found in bad meat, cheese or fruit

magic   an imaginary power that makes wonderful things happen that seem impossible, like changing a pumpkin into a beautiful coach

magician   someone who can do magic

magnet   a piece of iron or steel that has the power to pull other pieces of metal to it

magnificent   splendid; very grand

magpie   a black and white bird of the crow family. It is noisy and likes to collect bright shiny objects.

maid   an old-fashioned word for a girl or young woman. The same word is also used for a woman servant.

mail   anything that is sent through the post, such as letters and parcels

main   most important; chief

majesty   a title given to a king or queen

major   of great importance. The same word also means an officer in the army.

make   to produce, to build

make-up   face powder, lipstick and colouring used around the eyes

male   people and animals who can become fathers. Boys and men are of the male sex, but girls and women are of the female sex.

malt   grain prepared in a special way before it is made into beer

mammal   one of any kind of animal whose females have milk to feed their babies

mammoth   huge; enormous. The same word also means a huge hairy elephant that lived millions of years ago.

man   a male human being when he is grown up

manage   to look after or be responsible for something, such as a business or a household

manager   a person who is in charge of something, such as a business, a football club or a factory

mane   the long hair some animals have on their necks. Horses have manes and so do lions.

manger   a feeding box for animals, usually in a shed or stable

mangle   a machine with heavy rollers for squeezing water out of washing. The same word also means to tear or cut something to pieces in a very rough way.

mangold   a root vegetable, rather like a beetroot, used for feeding animals

mankind   all human beings

manners   how you behave towards other people, the way in which you do things. It is good manners to say please and thank you, but bad manners to snatch things and act in a rude way.

manor   the land belonging to a nobleman

mansion   a very large house

mantelpiece   a narrow shelf above the fireplace

manure   anything put into the ground to make plants and crops grow better

many a lot

map a special kind of drawing to show how to find your way about a place, a country or the different parts of the world

marble a hard kind of stone that is used in important buildings. Marble is also carved into statues and beautiful ornaments. The same word also means one of the round glass balls used in the game of marbles.

march to walk in step. Soldiers march in time to music in a parade.

mare a female horse

margarine a soft yellow food that looks like butter

margin a blank edge on the side of a page where nothing is printed

marigold a bright yellow or orange garden flower

marine to do with the sea. The same word also means a soldier serving on a ship.

marionette a puppet made to move by pulling strings

mark a spot or line on something

market a place, usually out of doors, where people meet to buy and sell food and other things

marmalade a kind of jam made from oranges, lemons or grapefruit cooked with sugar

maroon a dark brownish-red colour

marriage the ceremony by which a man and woman become husband and wife

marry   to become husband and wife

marsh   a piece of wet swampy land which is unsafe to walk on because your feet sink down into it

marshal   an important officer in the army. In the United States, the same word also means a sheriff.

marshmallow   a soft sticky white or pink sweet

marshy   wet; swampy

marvel   to wonder; to be amazed

marvellous   wonderful; splendid

marzipan   a sweet food made of crushed almonds and sugar

mascot   a person or animal or charm that is supposed to bring good luck

masculine   like, or to do with, men or boys

mash   to crush something so that it becomes soft and smooth, like mashed potatoes

mask   a cover to hide the face, sometimes funny, sometimes pretty and sometimes frightening

mass   a lump of something; a large quantity or number

massive   large and heavy

mast   a long pole that holds up the sails of a sailing vessel

master   someone who is in control or in command of other people

mat   a piece of thick material on a floor. Small mats are used on tables under hot plates.

match a small thin piece of wood or cardboard with a tip that makes fire

mate a friend or helper; someone you often play or work with

material what anything is made of

mathematics the study of numbers, measurements and quantities

matinée (*say matinay*) an afternoon performance of a show

mattress the thick soft part of the bed that you lie on

mauve a pale purple colour

may the pink or white blossom on a hawthorn tree

maybe another word for perhaps or possibly

mayor a man chosen to be leader of the town council

maypole a high pole set up on the first day of May. The pole is decorated with flowers and ribbons, and people dance around it.

maze a place with lots of paths that cross and turn into each other so that it is hard to find your way out

meadow a field of grass, often made into hay and used to feed animals

meal food eaten at certain times of the day. Breakfast, lunch, tea, dinner and supper are all meals.

mean   selfish and unkind. The same word is also used for explaining things, such as that the word *mean* means selfish and unkind.

meaning   the sense or explanation of something said or written

meanwhile   the time between two events or happenings

measles   an illness. You have a high fever and are covered in small itchy red spots.

measure   to find out the size or amount of anything

measurement   the size or amount of something

meat   the parts of animals that are cooked and eaten

mechanical   machine-like. A mechanical toy is worked by machinery, not by a person.

medal   a piece of metal like a coin or cross hanging on a ribbon. It is given as a reward for being very brave or very skilful.

meddle   to interfere with what someone else is trying to do

medicine   something that you eat or drink or rub on yourself to make you feel better when you are ill

medium   middle-sized

meek   gentle and patient; not likely to fight back or lose your temper easily

meet   to come together with someone or something

meeting   coming together for a purpose

melt   to turn to liquid when heated. Butter melts in warm weather and so does ice.

member   someone who belongs to a team or club or some other group of people

memory   the part of your mind that remembers things

men   more than one man

mend   to put something right; to repair it when it is torn or broken

mental   to do with the mind: worked out in your head and not written out

mention   to speak briefly about something

menu   a piece of card or paper with a list of what there is to eat in a restaurant or café

mercy   pity; forgiveness

meringue (*say merang*)   a white crisp food made from white of egg and sugar, whipped stiff and then baked in an oven

merit   to deserve something, such as a reward or punishment

mermaid   an imaginary sea creature, supposed to be half woman and half fish, with a fish tail instead of legs

merry   happy; enjoying yourself

merry-go-round   another word for roundabout

mess   an untidy muddle; confusion

message something you want a person who is not with you to know, so you write it down or ask another person to tell him

messenger someone who carries a message

metal hard materials like iron and steel. Cars and aeroplanes are mostly made of metal.

meteor a piece of rock travelling in space, often called a shooting star

meter an instrument for measuring a quantity of something, such as gas, water or electricity

method a way of doing something

metre a measure of length equal to 100 centimetres

mew the crying sound made by a cat or kitten

mice more than one mouse

microphone an instrument that picks up sounds for radio, television or tape recorders

microscope an instrument with a tube that you look through, which makes very tiny things look much larger

midday the middle of the day between morning and afternoon

middle halfway; in the centre

midget a person who is very small, even when grown up

midnight 12 o'clock at night, the middle of the night

midst another word for middle, when you mean in the middle of a crowd of people

mighty another word for powerful or strong

mild not strong or severe

mile a measure of distance equal to 1,760 yards

milk the white liquid that is used to feed babies. Most people drink cow's milk.

milkman a man who sells milk, or brings milk to your house

mill a machine for grinding things like grain, coffee beans and pepper into very small pieces. The same word also means a building or factory where cloth or steel is made.

millimetre a thousandth part of a metre

million a thousand times a thousand; 1,000,000

millionaire a very rich man who has a million pounds or more

mimic to imitate or copy someone else, usually in a mocking way

mince to chop or grind something, usually meat, into very small pieces

mincemeat a mixture of chopped-up fruit, nuts, raisins and other things, cooked in pastry, usually at Christmas time

mind what you think with. The same word also means to be careful and think what you are doing.

mine a large deep hole in the ground where men dig for coal, diamonds, gold or other minerals. The same word also means belonging to me.

miner a man who works in a mine

mineral any substance in the earth that can be dug out and used, such as coal, metal, rock

mingle to mix with or go about with, as when you mingle with the crowd at a football match

miniature a small copy of anything

minor not important. The same word also means a person who is not yet an adult.

mint a place where coins are made. The same word also means a small garden plant used for flavouring sauces and sweets.

minute One minute is 60 seconds. It takes 60 minutes to make an hour.

miracle something wonderful or fortunate that you would not expect to happen

mirage something you imagine you can see that is not really there, as when hot and thirsty travellers in the desert think they see water ahead

mirror a piece of glass with something behind it so that you can see yourself instead of seeing through the glass

misbehave to behave badly or in a rude way

mischief harm or damage; naughtiness

miser someone who hoards all his money and lives in a very poor way

miserable feeling very sad and unhappy

misery unhappiness; sorrow

misfortune bad luck; a calamity

miss to fail to hit, catch or find something

mist very low cloud

mistake something wrong, like a mistake in your sums

mistletoe an evergreen plant with pearly-looking berries, which grows on the branches of trees. It is used for decoration at Christmas.

mistrust not to trust or not to believe someone

misunderstand not to understand; to mistake the meaning of something

mite anything very small. In the old days there was a very small coin called a mite. The same word also means a kind of tiny insect.

mittens coverings for the hands, like gloves, but without places for the fingers

mix to put different things together

mixture two or more things put together

moan a long low sound made by someone in pain or sorrow

moat a big ditch, usually filled with water. In olden times, castles had deep moats around them so that enemies could not get across.

mock to make fun of someone

model a copy of something like a boat or aeroplane, usually smaller than the real thing. The same word also means someone who shows off clothes or someone who stays quite still so that artists can paint or draw pictures of them.

moderate fair; between bad and good

modern nowadays; at this time, not old-fashioned

moist damp; slightly wet

moisture dampness; slight wetness

mole a small animal with sharp claws, tiny eyes and dark thick fur. It digs long tunnels in the ground. The same word also means a small, dark spot on the skin.

moment a very short time

monarch a king, queen, emperor or empress

monastery a building where monks live

money coins and paper banknotes

mongrel a dog which is a mixture of different types

monitor a pupil in a school who is given a special job to help the teacher

monk a member of a religious group living in a monastery

monkey a small lively animal with a long tail. Monkeys live in hot countries, and are very good at climbing trees and swinging from branch to branch.

monster an enormous, horrible creature; a plant or animal of unusual or frightening appearance

month about 4 weeks. There are 12 months in a year.

monument a statue or building that is put up to make people remember someone or some event

mood how you feel in your mind. You can be in a good mood when you are happy, or in a bad mood when something has made you cross or unhappy.

moon the largest and brightest light we can see in the sky at night

moor a large open piece of land where nothing much grows except heather. The same word also means to fasten a boat or ship to the land.

mop pieces of sponge or thick cotton fastened on a long stick, used to clean floors or wash dishes

morning the time between dawn and midday

mortar a mixture of cement, sand and water used in building to make bricks stick together

mosaic a pattern or picture made by arranging lots of small pieces of coloured glass or stones

mosquito a small flying insect that bites

moss a very small green plant that looks like velvet. It grows close to the ground in damp places, especially in the woods.

moth an insect rather like a butterfly, except that it only flies at night. The grubs of some small moths eat holes in your clothes.

mother a woman who has a family

motor a machine which makes something work or move

motorbike a kind of heavy bicycle with a motor

motorway   a special road for fast traffic

motto   a short saying which gives a rule for behaviour, such as *Be prepared*

mould   a container into which you pour liquid that will get hard, and will have the shape of the container when you turn it out. The same word also means a green or grey furry covering that grows on stale bread or cheese.

mound   a heap of stones or earth; a small rounded hill

mount   another word for mountain. The same word also means to get up on something, like a horse or a bicycle.

mountain   a very high hill

mouse   a little animal with a long tail and sharp teeth

moustache (*say mustash*)   the hair that grows above a man's upper lip

mouth   the opening in your face which you use for speaking and eating

move   to go, or make something go, from one place to another

movement   the act of moving

mow (*rhymes with go*)   to cut grass or hay

much   a lot

muck   damp dirt or rubbish; manure

mud   soft wet earth

muddle   to make a mess of things; to do things in a confused way

mudguard a piece of metal over the wheels of a car or bicycle to stop the mud from splashing up

muff a tube-shaped piece of fur or warm material. You put your hands in through the openings to keep them warm.

muffin a soft cake, toasted and eaten with butter

muffler a woolly scarf

mug a large heavy cup with straight sides

mulberry a tree with berries something like raspberries. Mulberry leaves are the main food of silkworms.

mule an animal whose parents are a donkey and a horse

multiply to increase or make something a number of times larger

mumble to speak with your mouth nearly closed so that your words are not heard clearly

mumps a very uncomfortable illness. You have a fever, your neck swells up, and it hurts to swallow.

munch to chew with a crunching sound

municipal having to do with a city

murder to kill someone against the law of a country, not by accident or in wartime

murderer someone who kills another person against the law

murmur a gentle soft sound that goes on and on

muscle the fleshy parts of the body that tighten and loosen to make it move

museum   a place where interesting collections of things are set out for people to look at

mushroom   a small plant shaped like an umbrella. It can be cooked and eaten.

music   pleasing sounds that you sing or play on a musical instrument

must   to have to do something, such as going to school every day

mustard   a kind of browny-yellow paste, eaten with meat. It has a very strong flavour and makes your tongue feel hot.

mutiny   a refusal by soldiers, sailors or airmen to obey their officers

mutter   to speak so softly that it is hard to understand the words

mutton   the meat from sheep

muzzle   the jaws and nose of an animal. The same word also means a sort of cage or arrangement of straps fastened on an animal's nose and mouth to keep it from biting.

myself   me and no one else

mystery   something strange that has happened, but that cannot be explained or easily understood

myth   an old, old story which explains how something began or happened. The same word also means an imaginary person or event.

nag   to keep on scolding or finding fault

nail the hard part at the end of a finger or toe. The same word also means a thin sharp piece of metal used to join pieces of wood.

naked without clothes or covering

name what a person or thing is called

nanny-goat a female goat

nap a short sleep

napkin a square piece of cloth or paper used to wipe your mouth and fingers when you are eating

narcissus a spring flower, white or yellow, that smells very sweet

narrow slim; thin; not wide

nasturtium a plant with lots of round leaves and orange, red and yellow coloured flowers

nasty not nice; not pleasant

nation all the people living in one country under one government

national belonging to one nation or country

native a person born in a particular place or country

natural not man-made

nature everything in the world that is not man-made

naughty not doing what you should; behaving badly

navigate to steer or guide a ship or aeroplane

navy a nation's warships and the sailors who run them

near   close to; not far away

nearly   very closely; almost; not far from

neat   tidy; in good order

necessary   having to be done; needed

neck   the part of your body between your head and your shoulders

necklace   a string of beads or thin chain worn round the neck

nectar   a sweet juice found in some flower blossoms

need   to have to have something. You need clothes to keep you warm.

needle   a long, thin pointed piece of metal used for sewing. There are also special needles for knitting.

negative   meaning or saying *no*

neglect   to forget or be careless about looking after something

neigh   the cry a horse makes, usually when it is frightened or excited

neighbour   a person who lives near you

neither   not one or the other

nephew   the son of a brother or sister

nerve   one of the small thread-like parts of your body that carries messages to and from the brain so that you can move and feel. The same word also means courage and daring.

nervous   jumpy; easily frightened

nest a bird's home, where the eggs are laid and hatched out

net pieces of string knotted together so that there are more holes than string

netball a game played by two teams. A large ball is thrown into a small net on a pole.

nettle a weed with prickly hairs that sting if they touch your skin

never not ever; not at any time

new only just made; not old; not seen before

newborn just born

news things that have just happened

newspaper a printed daily or weekly paper that tells you about things that have just happened

newt a small animal like a lizard that can live on land as well as in water

next the nearest; the one after

nib the metal point of a pen

nibble to eat with tiny bites

nice kind; friendly; pretty; pleasant

nick a little cut in something

nickel a silvery-grey metal

nickname a name you give to someone for fun, to describe what he is like, such as *shorty* for someone who is not very tall

niece the daughter of a brother or sister

nigh another word for near

night the time between sunset and sunrise, when the sky is dark

nightdress a garment worn in bed by girls and women

nightgown another word for nightdress

nightingale a small brown bird whose song is even more beautiful at night than in the daytime

nimble quick or clever in moving or climbing

nip to pinch or bite off a little bit of something

no the opposite of yes. The same word also means not any.

noble great; grand

nobleman a man of high rank

nobody no one; no person

nod to bend your head forward and back to show you agree. The same word also means to let your head fall forward when you are sleepy.

noise a sound, sometimes very loud

nomad one of a group of people who have no permanent home, but who roam about looking for food for themselves and their animals

none not one; not any

nonsense talk which means nothing

noon 12 o'clock in the day; midday

noose a loop in a rope, with a slip-knot that can be tightened by pulling it

normal ordinary; usual

north the direction which is the opposite of south, on your left as you face the rising sun

nose the part of your face with which you smell, and through which you breathe

nosey wanting to know all about other people's belongings and activities

nostril one of the two openings in your nose

note a short letter. The same word also means a sound in music or a piece of paper money.

notebook a little book in which you write things down that you don't want to forget

nothing not anything

notice to see something. The same word also means a printed piece of paper announcing something.

nought nothing; zero

nourish to feed

novel new and different. The same word also means a long story about imaginary people.

novelty something new and different

now at this time

nowhere not anywhere or any place

nozzle a spout at the end of a pipe or hose

nude naked; without clothing

nudge   to poke or push someone gently with your elbow

nuisance   something or someone who gets in the way of what others want to do

numb   not able to feel, as when your fingers are numb with cold

number   a word which says how many. One (1), two (2), three (3), and four (4) are numbers.

numeral   a figure, a number such as 1, 2 or 3

numerous   very many

nun   a female member of a religious group living in a convent

nurse   someone who helps the doctor to look after people who are ill

nursery   a room or building where very young children sleep or play

nut   a fruit or seed with a hard shell. The same word also means a piece of metal with a hole through it that you screw on to the end of a bolt.

nutmeg   a hard spicy seed used to flavour food

nylon   a man-made material used for making clothing, brushes and other useful things

oak   a kind of tree that can grow very big and lives to a very old age. It has acorns as its fruit.

oar   a long piece of wood with one flat end, used to row a boat

oasis   a place in a desert where plants and trees grow because there is water

oath a solemn promise that you will speak the truth or keep your word

oats a kind of grain used mostly to feed animals. Oats are also ground up and cooked with water to make porridge.

obedience doing as you are told

obey to do as you are told

object a thing; something you can see or handle. The same word also means to disagree with someone else's idea.

oblige to force someone to do something. The same word also means to do someone a favour.

oblong a squared shape with four straight sides. Two opposite sides are of equal length and the other sides are also equal but longer or shorter than the first two.

observe to watch carefully; to notice

obstacle anything that stands in the way so that you cannot go forward

obstinate wanting your own way; stubborn

obtain another word for get

occasion a particular event or happening

occupation the kind of work that you do

occupy to live in, as when a family occupies a house. The same word also means to go into enemy land in wartime and take over towns and cities.

occur to happen

ocean a very big sea

o'clock   the time by the clock

octopus   a sea creature with eight arms covered with suckers

odd   strange; queer. The same word also means not even in number (1, 3, 5, 7, 9 are odd numbers).

odour   smell

offence   a crime. The same word also means something that hurts someone's feelings or makes him angry.

offend   to do something wrong; to displease; to make someone angry

offensive   causing hurt; unpleasant

offer   to say you will do or give something

office   a building or room where people work with business papers

officer   someone who commands others, as in the army, navy or air force

often   many times; happening over and over again

oil   a thick greasy liquid which can come from animals or plants, or from under the ground

ointment   a soothing paste you put on sores or cuts

O.K.   all right

old   having been alive or on earth for a long time

olden   long ago, as when we say in olden days or in olden times

older   having lived longer than someone else, or existed longer than something else

old-fashioned   of times long ago; not modern

omelette   eggs beaten up, fried until the mixture is almost solid, and then folded over

omit   to leave out; not to do something

once   for one time only; at a time long ago

onion   a bulb-like vegetable with a strong smell and flavour

only   single; one and no more

open   not shut; able to let things through

opening   an open place; a hole or space

operation   something that is done, especially something done by doctors in a hospital to make people well again

opinion   what you think about something

opportunity   a chance to do something

opposite   as different as possible from something else; across from

optical   having to do with eyes or with seeing

orange   a sweet fruit. The same word also means the colour of the fruit.

orangutan   a large reddish-brown ape that lives in jungles

orbit the path in which something moves around another thing in space

orchard a lot of fruit trees growing together

order a command. The same word also means to ask for something to be done, such as for something to be sent to you from a shop.

ordinary usual; not special or different

ore rock or mineral from which we get metal

organ a large musical instrument with a keyboard and pipes that the sounds come from

organization a group of people or of nations who get together to work for a particular purpose; such as the World Health Organization

organize to get a group of people together for a particular purpose: to plan and arrange something

ornament anything used to make something look prettier, such as jewellery or a vase

orphan a child whose mother and father are both dead

ostrich a very large bird which has long legs but which cannot fly because its wings are too small

otherwise if not; if things are different

otter a furry web-footed swimming animal rather like a large weasel

ought must; should

ounce a measurement of weight. There are 16 ounces in a pound.

outburst a sudden bursting out, such as cheering when a goal is scored at a football match

outfit a set of clothing or equipment

outing a pleasure trip or walk

outlaw a person who fights against the law and is told that he cannot be protected by the law. Robin Hood and his men were outlaws.

outline a line drawn to show the shape of something round the outside edge. The same word also means the main ideas of a story or a plan.

outside the opposite of inside; out of doors

oval egg-shaped. A rugby football is oval.

oven the inside part of a stove where you bake things

overall a piece of clothing worn over other clothes to keep them clean

overcoat an outdoor coat worn over all your other clothes

overcome to get the better of someone or something; to defeat

overflow to spill over the top of a container because it is too full

overhang to hang out over; to stick out over

overtake to catch up with and go in front of someone or something

overthrow to destroy or defeat completely

owe   to need to pay for something you have bought

owl   a bird with big eyes and a sharp curved beak. Owls fly at night and sleep through the day.

own   to have something that belongs to you

oyster   a shellfish with a very hard flat shell in two parts

oxen   bulls and cows

pace   a step or the length of a step, as when you say something is six paces away

pack   to put things into a container. You pack clothes into a trunk or suitcase when you go away. The same word also means a bundle of things carried on your back.

package   a parcel or bundle

packet   a small parcel or package

pad   a lot of sheets of paper glued or sewn together at the top. The same word also means a piece of thick, soft material, usually to protect a part of your body from harm.

paddle   to walk around in water up to your ankles. The same word also means a pole with a broad part at the end, which you use to move a canoe through the water.

page   one side of a sheet of paper in a book, newspaper, magazine or notebook. The same word also means a young boy who attends a bride at her wedding, or who runs errands in a hotel.

pageant   a show in costume, usually about things that happened long ago

pail   another word for bucket

pain   the feeling when something hurts you

paint   to colour something with a brush and coloured liquid called paint

painting   a coloured picture painted on paper or canvas

pair   two things which are meant to be used together, like a pair of shoes

palace   the house where a king or queen lives

pale   not having much colour or brightness; looking washed out

paling   one of the pieces of wood in a special kind of fence

palm   the inside of your hand between your fingers and your wrist. The same word also means a tall tree with large fan-shaped leaves at the top. It grows in hot countries.

pan   a metal container with a handle, used for cooking

pancake   a thin round cake eaten hot. You cook it in a frying pan.

panda   a large black and white wild animal, something like a bear. Some pandas are much smaller and look rather like a large cat with a bushy tail and a pointed nose.

panic   sudden fear or terror that keeps people from thinking reasonably

pansy   a small garden plant with velvety, brightly coloured flowers

pant   to gasp for breath

panther   a kind of leopard

pantomime   a musical play for children, usually a fairy tale. The same word also means a play in which the actors do not speak.

pantry   a small room or cupboard where food is kept

pants   trousers

paper   the material used to write on or wrap parcels in

parable   a fable or story that is meant to show you how to behave towards others

parachute   a large piece of strong cloth which is fastened to a man who is going to jump from an aeroplane. It opens like an umbrella, and brings him safely and slowly to the ground.

parade   a lot of people walking or marching together, sometimes in costume

paraffin   a kind of oil that is burned in stoves and lamps

parallel   going in the same direction the same distance apart and never meeting, like a pair of railway lines

parcel   a bundle of things, usually tied up in paper

parchment   the skin of a goat, sheep or other animal, cleaned and dried. In olden days, before paper was invented, it was used to write on.

pardon to forgive

parent a mother or a father

parish a part of a county with its own church

park an open space with grass and trees and
playgrounds for children. The same word also
means to stop a car and leave it at the side
of the street or in a parking space.

parliament a group of men and women who are
chosen to make the laws for the people in a
country

parlour another word for living-room

parrot a brightly-coloured bird often kept as a pet
in a cage. Some parrots can imitate talking.

parsnip a vegetable with a thick whitish root
shaped rather like a carrot

part a piece of something. The same word also
means to leave someone.

particle a tiny bit or piece of something

particular single or special. The same word also
means fussy or very careful.

partner a person who shares equally, or who plays
or works with another person

partridge a plump wild bird rather like a small
pheasant

party a lot of people all together having a good
time

pass to move ahead of something in front of you.
The same word also means to hand something
to someone.

passage   a long narrow part inside a building, with doors opening at the sides and end of it

passenger   someone who rides in a vehicle but who is not the driver

passport   special papers from the government that help you to travel in other countries

paste   a thick white liquid, used to stick paper and other things together. The same word also means a thick food which is spread on bread or toast for flavour.

pastime   a game or hobby that you like to do to pass the time

pastry   a mixture of flour and water and fat which is rolled flat before it is baked

pasture   a field where sheep and cattle are allowed to eat the grass

pat   to hit something very lightly

patch   a small piece of cloth used to cover a hole in clothes. The same word also means a small piece of ground.

pate   the top of the head

patent   a government paper that keeps other people from using an invention without permission

path   a narrow way along which people may travel, usually on foot

patience   the ability to wait for something without making a fuss

patient   able to wait for something without making a fuss; taking a lot of trouble to get something right. The same word also means a sick person who is being looked after by a doctor.

patter to tap lightly and quickly. Rain patters on the roof.

pattern curved or straight lines repeated many times over, as on a patterned carpet or wallpaper. The same word also means a model or plan to help you make something, like a dress pattern.

pause to stop what you are doing for a moment

pavement a hard path at the side of the street for people to walk safely

pavilion a large tent or a wooden building, usually for the players on a sports ground

paw the foot of a four-legged animal which has claws

pay to give money for something you have bought or for work someone has done

pea one of the round green seeds which are used as food. Peas grow in pods on a climbing plant.

peace a time when no one is fighting

peach a juicy round fruit with a velvety skin and a stone-like seed

peacock a large bird with beautifully-coloured feathers. He can spread his tail out like a large fan.

peak the topmost point. The same word also means the brim of a cap that sticks out in front.

peal a loud sound, as of bells ringing, or of thunder

peanut   a nut which grows underground in a pod. Sometimes peanuts are called monkey nuts because monkeys are very fond of them.

pear   a juicy fruit rather like an apple, only softer and rather cone-shaped

pearl   a small creamy-white jewel, used for necklaces and other jewellery. Pearls grow inside some oyster shells.

pebble   a small smooth roundish piece of stone

peck   to pick up food in the beak with short jerky movements. Hens peck at their food.

peculiar   odd; strange; unusual

pedal   a foot lever to make something work. Bicycles have pedals and so have pianos.

pedestrian   someone who is walking

peel   the skin of fruit or vegetables. You can peel bark off trees and sometimes pieces of your skin when you have been sunburned.

peep   to take a quick look

peer   a nobleman, usually with the rank of Lord. The same word also means to look very closely.

peg   a strong clip or pin used to hang things up— like washing on a line, or to fasten things down —like a tent rope

pekinese   a small, fluffy dog with almost no nose

pelican a big water-bird which has a large pouch under the lower part of its beak. It can scoop up fish in its pouch, and store them there until it wants to eat.

pellet a tiny ball of something, such as paper, clay or metal

pelt the skin or hide of an animal. The same word also means to throw something, such as snowballs, or to pour down, like heavy rain.

pen a tool used for writing with ink

penalty a punishment for breaking a rule

pence more than one penny

pencil a thin tool for writing and drawing. It is made of wood with a stick of black or coloured material in the middle.

pendulum a weight on the end of a rod that swings from side to side as in a clock

penguin a web-footed swimming bird that lives near the South Pole. It has short legs and wings but cannot fly.

penknife a small knife that you can carry in your pocket

penny a piece of money

people men, women, boys and girls

pepper a spicy powder used to flavour food. It tastes hot, and can make you sneeze if you breathe it in. The same word also means a bright green or red vegetable that grows in hot countries.

peppermint   a green plant used for flavouring
sauces, drinks and sweets

perch   something a bird sits or stands on, like a
stick or twig

percussion   all those musical instruments, such as a
drum or cymbals, that are banged or struck

perfect   without any faults or mistakes

perform   to do or act: to play a part on the stage or
to play a musical instrument

performance   an act: a play or other entertainment

perfume   a sweet smell; a liquid having a sweet
smell

perhaps   possibly; maybe

peril   great danger

perimeter   the outside measurement of a figure or
area

period   a length of time

periscope   a tube containing mirrors used in
submarines or underground so that people can
see what is going on above them

perish   to die or be destroyed

permanent   long-lasting, not ever changing. A perm,
a short word for permanent wave, keeps hair
curly for a long time.

permission   freedom given to do something, as when
you are given permission to stay up especially
late to watch television

permit   to allow; to give permission

persist   to keep on trying to do something or asking for something

person   a man, woman or child

personal   belonging to one person

perspire   to give off sweat from your skin when you are very hot

persuade   to talk someone into doing something, even if he doesn't want to

pest   something or someone that makes difficulties for others; a nuisance

pet   an animal that is kept at home; not wild. Dogs and cats are pets.

petal   the part of a flower that grows out from the middle

petrel   a small seabird with long wings

petrol   short for petroleum; a kind of liquid oil used to make motor engines work

petticoat   a skirt worn under dresses by girls and women

petty   small; unimportant

pew   a long wooden bench with a back, for people to sit on in church

pheasant   a bird, usually wild, with beautiful long tail feathers

phone   short for telephone

photograph   a picture taken with a camera

phrase   a group of words, usually part of a sentence

physical to do with nature or with the body. Physical Education (P.E.) exercises your muscles.

piano a large musical instrument with a keyboard

pick to choose; to gather. The same word also means a sharp tool used to break rock or hard ground.

pickle to keep in vinegar cooked vegetables like beetroot and cucumbers

picnic an outing when you take food to eat out of doors

picture a drawing, painting or photograph

pie food made of pastry outside, and filled with fruit or meat

piece a part or bit of something, but not all of it, like a piece of pie. The word also means one of something, like a piece of paper.

pier a platform of stone, wood or metal, that reaches out over the water so that ships and boats can stop at the end of it

pierce to make a hole with something sharp

pig a fat farm animal with a curly tail

pigeon a plump bird with short legs, that makes a cooing sound. Some pigeons are kept as pets and some are used to carry messages or for racing.

pigmy   one of a tribe of very small people who live in the jungles of some hot countries. The word can also be spelled pygmy.

pigsty   a place where pigs are kept

pigtail   a braid or plait of hair hanging from the back of the head

pike   a large greedy freshwater fish. The same word also means a weapon like a spear, used in the old days.

pile   a lot of things on top of each other, like a pile of books, or a pile of old junk

pilgrim   someone who travels a long way to visit a holy place

pill   medicine like a little ball or pellet, that must be swallowed

pillar   a large post of stone or wood, used to hold up part of a building

pillion   a seat on a motor cycle, behind the driver

pillow   a bag filled with feathers or some soft material, where you lay your head in bed

pillowcase   a covering for a pillow. The word pillowslip has the same meaning.

pilot   a man who steers a ship into harbour or who controls an aeroplane

pimple   a small pointed swelling on the skin

pin   a thin pointed piece of metal used for fastening or holding things together

pinafore   an overall to keep your clothes clean; a sleeveless dress worn over a blouse or jumper

pincers a small tool used for holding things steady or pulling nails out of wood

pinch to squeeze something tightly, usually between finger and thumb

pine an evergreen tree with cones and leaves like needles

pineapple a sweet-tasting fruit that looks something like a large pine cone. It grows in hot countries.

pink a very pale red colour. The same word also means a garden flower with a sweet spicy smell.

pint a measure for liquid

pip a fruit seed

pipe any tube, usually of metal, through which a liquid (such as water) or gas flows. The same word also means a small bowl on the end of a tube, used for smoking tobacco.

pirate someone who robs ships at sea

pistol a small hand gun that can be carried in the pocket

pit a hole in the ground

pitch to throw or fall forward: to set something up, such as a tent or a stall in a market. The same word also means the highness or lowness of musical notes.

pitcher a person who throws a ball in some games. The same word also means a large jug for holding or pouring liquids.

pitchfork   a tool used for lifting hay

pity   a feeling of sadness you have because someone else is ill or unhappy

pivot   the pin or centre on which something turns

pixie   a kind of fairy

placard   a written or printed poster or notice

place   somewhere where something is

plague   a terrible illness that spreads from person to person very quickly

plaice   a flat sea fish that is good to eat

plaid (*rhymes with sad*)   a piece of woollen cloth with a checked or tartan pattern

plain   ordinary; not fancy or decorated. The same word also means a large flat part of the country.

plait (*rhymes with mat*)   several pieces of ribbon, straw or hair twisted under and over each other, like a rope

plan   to think out how a thing can be done before you do it. The same word also means a model or drawing showing the shape and design of something, like a building or a town.

plane   a carpenter's tool used to make wood smooth. It is also a short word for aeroplane.

planet   anything in the sky which, like the earth, goes round the sun

plank   a long flat heavy piece of wood, thicker than a board

plant   anything that grows up from the earth, like grass or flowers

plaster   a mixture of water, sand and lime, which hardens when it is put on walls and ceilings. The same word also means a piece of sticky tape that holds a bandage in place.

plastic   material that can be moulded into different shapes when it is soft. Later it becomes hard. Lots of things are made of plastic, such as combs, cups and buckets.

plasticine   a soft clay-like substance that doesn't ever get hard. It is used for modelling.

plate   a round flat dish for food

platform   the raised part of a hall or theatre for the speakers or actors. The same word also means the part of a railway station beside the tracks, where you get on to a train.

play   to have fun: to take part in a game: to perform on a musical instrument. The same word also means a show acted on a stage, usually without music.

playground   a special place at school or in a park where children can play

playmate   someone you play with

playtime   a period of time for playing, not working or studying

pleasant   nice; agreeable; enjoyable

please   to make someone feel happy. You also use this word when you are being polite in asking someone to do something.

pleasure   a feeling of being glad and happy when you are enjoying yourself

pleat   a fold in cloth, pressed or stitched down to keep it in place

plenty   more than enough; all that is needed

pliers   a tool, like small pincers, used to twist or bend wire

plimsolls   canvas shoes with rubber soles

plod   to walk heavily and slowly

plot   a small piece of land. The same word also means the main happenings in a play or story. Sometimes it means a wicked or evil plan, like the Gunpowder Plot.

plough   a farm tool pulled along by horses or a tractor. It cuts into the ground and turns it over.

pluck   courage; bravery. The same word also means to pull at the strings of a musical instrument, such as the guitar.

plug   a piece of metal or rubber made to fit a hole so the water doesn't run out. An electric plug fits into a socket to obtain electric power.

plum   a juicy fruit with a stone in the middle

plumber   a man who connects up or mends water pipes

plume   a large curly feather, sometimes worn as an ornament on a hat

plump   rather fat and well-rounded

plunge   to throw yourself into water; to rush into something

plural   more than one. The plural of cat is cats.

plus   the sign + which shows that numbers are to be
added

plywood   very thin layers of wood glued together

pneumonia (*say newmonia*)   a painful illness of the
lungs

poach   to cook foods, such as eggs without their
shells, or fish, in very hot water. The same
word also means to catch animals or fish on
someone else's land without his permission.

pocket   a little bag sewn into clothes to put things in

pod   the outside covering of seeds

poem   a piece of writing, like a song without music,
that shows your thoughts and imaginings

poet   someone who writes poems

poetry   the art of writing poetry. The same word
also means poems as in *a book of poetry*.

point   the sharp end of something, like a pin or a
pencil

pointed   sharp; with a point; like the end of a pin

poison   something swallowed or injected that can
make you very ill or even kill you

poke   to jab or push anything suddenly

poker   a metal rod used for stirring a fire. The same
word is the name of a card game.

polar   having to do with the North and South Poles.
Polar bears live near the North Pole.

pole   a long rounded piece of wood or metal, used

to hold something up, such as a flag. The same word also means the north or south ends of the world's axis.

police   a group of men and women whose job is to see that the laws of the country are obeyed. If you see someone breaking the law, you can ask the police to do something about it.

polish   to make something shiny by rubbing it hard, usually with special powder, paste or liquid

polite   having good manners

pollen   yellow powder in the middle of flowers

poncho   an outer garment like a blanket with a hole in the middle for the head to go through

pond   a small lake

pony   a little horse

poodle   a kind of dog with very curly hair

pool   a small area of water, sometimes no bigger than a puddle

poor   having little money or few belongings. The same word also means not good, like poor soil where nothing grows very well.

pop   a sharp quick exploding sound. The same word can be short for popular. Then it means music or art that most people like.

popcorn   a special kind of corn that makes a popping sound and bursts open when it is heated

poplar   a tall, straight, narrow tree

poppy   a plant, usually with bright red flowers, often seen growing wild in the fields in summer

popular   liked by most people

population   the people, or the number of people living in any country, city, town or village

porch   a covered entrance to a building

porcupine   a wild animal with a coat of quills mixed with hairs

pork   pigmeat

porpoise   a sea animal, rather like a small whale with a blunt snout

porridge   a cooked breakfast food made from ground-up oats

port   a harbour, or a town with a harbour

porter   a man who carries your luggage. The same word also means someone who lets people in or out of a door or a gate at the entrance to a building.

portion   a part; a helping of food

portrait   a painting or drawing of a person

positive   meaning yes: absolutely sure

possess   to own or to have

possible   able to be done

post   a long piece of wood or metal, fastened in the ground so that it stands up straight. The same word also means letters and parcels sent and delivered; another word for mail.

postcard a piece of thin cardboard on which you can write to your friends. Most postcards have a picture on the back.

poster a large notice or picture that tells you about something that is going to happen. Some posters show you pictures of things you can buy, like food or clothes.

postman a man who collects and delivers the post

post office the place where you buy stamps and licences. It is also the place where all letters and parcels are sorted before they are delivered.

postpone to put off to another time

posy a small bunch of flowers

pot any deep dish for cooking. The same word also means plastic or clay containers for plants.

potato a vegetable that grows under the ground

potter someone who makes pots and other things out of clay. The same word also means to do things in a rather lazy way.

pottery crockery, ornaments and other things made out of baked clay

pouch a small bag

pouffe a large floor cushion to sit on, or to put your feet on

pounce to spring or jump down on something suddenly

pound a measure of weight: a piece of paper money. The same word also means to hit something with very heavy blows, like pounding on a locked door.

pour to make liquid run out of a container by tipping it forward

pout to close your lips and push them out to show that you are not pleased

powder very tiny dustlike bits of something. Flour and cocoa are powders.

power ability to do something; strength

practical useful

practice something done over and over until you are good at it, like throwing a ball, or playing a musical instrument

practise to do something often, so that you become good at it

prairie a large area of flat grassy land with very few trees

praise to say very nice things about someone or something

pram a four-wheeled vehicle for babies and very young children, pushed by hand. The word is short for perambulator.

pray to ask God for help; to request humbly

prayer the act of praying

preach to speak to others about being good, usually in church

precious very valuable; worth a lot of money

precipice a steep cliff

preface a short beginning to a book to explain what it is about

prefer to like one thing better than another

prefix a syllable at the beginning of a word which changes its meaning. If you put *un* before the word *pleasant* it changes the meaning to *not pleasant.*

pregnant carrying a baby or babies not yet born

prepare to make or get something ready

present something that is given to you. The same word also means at this time; now.

president the chief person in the government of a country that hasn't a king or queen. The same word can also mean the most important man in a club or business.

press to push against or push down. The same word also means all newspapers and magazines and the people who write what is printed in them.

pressure force or weight pushing against something

pretend to make believe

pretty lovely; beautiful

prevent to stop something from happening

previous happening or occurring before some other event

prey a bird or animal that is hunted for food by another bird or animal

price how much money you have to pay for something

prick   to make a tiny hole with something sharp. You must be careful not to prick your finger with a needle when you are sewing.

prickle   a sharp point growing on the stem of a plant or on an animal. The thorns on a rosebush are prickles, and so are the stiff hairs on a hedgehog.

pride   a high opinion of how clever you are and how nice you look. Sometimes it means a feeling of pleasure about something you have done well.

priest   a man in charge of a church who leads the prayers there

primary   first of all

primrose   a small pale yellow wildflower that is one of the earliest to bloom in spring

prince   the son of a king or queen

princess   the daughter of a king or queen

print   to press words and pictures on paper with a heavy machine

prison   a place where people who do things against the law have to stay for a period of time

prisoner   someone who has been captured in war or who is locked up in a prison because he has done something wrong

private   belonging to one person or group of people. The same word also means a soldier in the army.

prize   a reward for doing something well

probable   likely to happen

problem a question that is difficult to answer or decide

proceed to go ahead; to go on

procession a large number of people or vehicles moving along in a line

prod to poke

produce to make; to cause; to bring into being

producer someone who produces something, especially a film or play

profession a kind of work that needs special study and training, such as the nursing profession or the teaching profession

profit gain; the money left over after you have paid all your expenses

programme a printed paper giving information about a performance

progress movement forward or onward; improvement

prohibit to forbid or prevent

promenade a public footpath in a park or at the seaside where you walk for pleasure

promise to say that you will or will not do something, without fail

prompt quick; at once; with no delay

prong one of the sharp spikes on a fork

pronounce to speak or sound out words

proof a way of showing that what is said is true

prop   a long piece of wood or metal that is put under something to keep it from falling down

propel   to drive forward

propeller   the part of a ship or aeroplane that drives it forward

proper   right; as it should be

properly   in the right way

property   something that belongs to someone

prophecy   what someone says will happen in the future

prophesy   to say what will happen in the future

propose   to suggest something, such as a plan of action or way of going about things

prosecute   to speak against someone in a court of law because he is supposed to have done something wrong

protect   to guard or defend

protest   to object to something; to disagree

proud   having a feeling of pride; pleased that you are good at something

prove   to show that what is said is true

proverb   a well-known short saying which is often used to show you how you should act, like *Least said soonest mended*

provide to supply; to give what is needed

prowl to move about silently and secretly

pry to peer into or try to find out about things that do not concern you

pub a place where beer and other drinks are sold. The word is short for public house.

public open to or belonging to everyone; the opposite of private

pudding any soft, sweet food eaten at the end of a meal. Some puddings are made with meat, and eaten as the main part of a meal.

puddle a small pool of water, usually left in the road after it has been raining

puff to blow air or smoke out of the mouth. The same word also means a soft piece of material used to put powder on the skin.

puffin a sea bird with a short thick beak

pull to get hold of something and bring it towards you

pulley a wheel with a hollow rim. You put a rope around the rim and pull on it to lift heavy things.

pullover a knitted garment with sleeves

pump a machine used to get water from a well. The same word also means the machine you use to put air into tyres.

pumpkin a large yellow- or orange-coloured fruit that grows on a vine on the ground

punch   to hit hard, usually with your fists

punctual   on time; not late

punctuate   to divide writing into phrases or sentences by using special marks, such as a full-stop (.), question mark (?) or comma (,)

puncture   to make a hole in something

punish   to make someone suffer or pay for doing something wrong

punishment   something that makes a person suffer or pay for wrong-doing

punt   a small flat-bottomed boat that is square at both ends

pupil   a person who is taught by a teacher. The same word also means the round dark circle in the middle of your eye through which you see.

puppet   a doll which can be moved by pulling strings or putting your hand inside it

puppy   a young dog

purchase   to buy something

pure   clean; without fault

purl   a knitting stitch, the opposite to plain stitch

purple   a colour made by mixing red and blue

purpose   something you plan to do

purr   the sound a cat makes when it is happy

purse   a small bag to keep money in

pursue   to go after, to follow

push to move something away from you without lifting it

pushchair a small chair on wheels, for a young child to ride in

put to place something

puzzle a kind of game or question. You have to think very hard to get the answer.

pygmy one of a tribe of very small people who live in the jungles of some hot countries. The word can also be spelled pigmy.

pyjamas a sleeping suit

pylon a metal tower or mast that holds up electric cables

pyramid a solid shape with flat triangular sides, usually on a square base

python a large dangerous snake that can kill people by squeezing them in its coils

quack the noise a duck makes

quail a wild bird like a small partridge. The same word also means to lose courage.

quaint old-fashioned; a little odd

quake to tremble, shake or quiver

quality how good or bad something is. Clothes of good quality usually cost more but will last longer than clothes of poor quality.

quantity   the size, number or amount of things

quarrel   to argue or disagree with someone in an angry way

quarry   a place where stone for building is dug out. The same word also means an animal that is being hunted.

quart   a measure of liquid equal to two pints

quarter   one-fourth of anything, a fourth part

quay (*say kee*)   a landing place for boats or ships

queen   a woman who is the ruler of a country, or the wife of a king

queer   odd; strange; not ordinary

quench   to put an end to something, as when you quench your thirst by having a drink, or when you quench a fire by putting water on it

query   a question

question   something someone wants to know

queue (*say kew*)   a line of people waiting their turn. The same word also means a pigtail at the back of the head.

quick   fast; in a very short time

quiet   not making a noise; silent; at rest

quill   the hard stiff part of a feather: one of the sharp spines on some animals, such as hedgehogs

quilt   a thick padded bedcover

quit   to leave; to go away

quiver   to tremble or shiver

quiz   a lot of questions to find out how much someone knows

quoit   a heavy flat ring which you try to throw on to a peg

rabbit   a small furry animal with long ears. Some rabbits are kept in hutches as pets, but wild rabbits dig holes in the ground to live in.

race   to move very quickly to get to a place before someone else does. The same word also means a large group of people having a similar appearance, especially the same skin colour. Europeans, Africans and Chinese all belong to different races.

racetrack   the path or course where a race is run

rack   a framework to keep things on, such as a hat rack

racket   a bat with a network of strings used in playing tennis and other games. Sometimes the word is spelled racquet. The same word also means a loud noise.

radiant   bright; sending out rays of heat or light. The same word also means showing joy.

radiate   to send out rays of heat or light: to spread out in many directions from a centre

radiator   a set of pipes or other apparatus used to heat a room by electricity, hot water or steam. The same word also means the part of a car that holds water to keep the engine from getting too hot.

radio an instrument that brings broadcast music and other people's voices through the air from far away

radish the small red and white root of a plant, used in salads

radius a straight line from the centre of a circle to its outer edge

raffia strips of palm leaves used to make things such as mats and baskets

raft floating logs or boards fastened together

rag a piece of cloth that is old and often full of holes

rage great anger; fury

raid a quick surprise attack

rail a wooden or metal bar used as part of a fence: a long metal bar which is used to make a railway track

railing a fence of posts and rails

railway very long parallel bars of metal that make a road or track for trains to run on

rain drops of water that fall out of the clouds

rainbow a beautifully-coloured arch that you can see in the sky when the sun shines through rain

raincoat a coat made of rubber or some other material that doesn't let the rain through

rainfall the amount of rain that falls in a certain period of time

raise to lift up. The same word means to collect,

as when you raise money for charity. It also means to grow or breed something, like plants or animals.

raisin a dried grape used in cakes and puddings

rake a garden tool with a long handle and metal teeth

ram a male sheep. The same word also means to push hard or crash into something.

ramble to stroll about for pleasure. The same word also means a long walk in the country.

ranch a very big farm where large numbers of cattle, horses or sheep are raised

ranger a man who is paid to look after a forest or large area of land

rank the position of a soldier, sailor or airman in the armed forces. The same word also means a row or line of things or people.

ransack to search through something in a rather rough and untidy way

ransom a sum of money paid for the safe return of someone who has been captured or kidnapped

rap to hit sharply

rapid quick; speedy

rapids a rocky, steep part of a river where the water flows very quickly

rapier a long thin sword

rare unusual; valuable

rascal a dishonest person; one who makes mischief or who cannot be trusted

rash an outbreak of red spots on the skin. The same word also means acting hastily, without careful thought.

raspberry a small soft red fruit with lots of seeds

rat an animal like a large mouse, with long sharp teeth

rate how fast something happens. The same word also means how much you pay for something.

rather somewhat; to some extent

ration a share or portion. When there is not enough food to go round, everyone is allowed the same ration, so that everyone has a fair share.

rattle the noise you hear when you shake hard things together

rattlesnake a poisonous snake with rattling bony rings on its tail

raw not cooked

ray a thin line of light, like a sunbeam

rayon a man-made silky material. Dresses, blouses, ties and other clothes are often made of rayon.

razor a very sharp instrument, used to shave hair off

reach to stretch out far enough to touch or get hold of something. The same word also means to get to a place; to arrive.

read to understand printed or written words

ready able to do something at once; prepared

eal   true; not made up or imaginary

ealize   to understand clearly

eally   without question; in fact

eap   to cut and gather in crops of grain

ear   the back part

eason   why something is done or said; an explanation

easonable   sensible; fair; good enough

ebel   to go against someone in authority

eceipt   a written or printed note that proves you have paid for something

eceive   to take something that is given or sent to you

ecent   happening a short time ago

ecess   a place set back in a wall. The same word also means a short rest from work or lessons.

ecipe (*say ressipee*)   information that tells you how to cook something and what to put in it

ecite   to say something aloud that you have learned by heart, like reciting a poem

eckless   careless; not thinking or caring about what could happen

eckon   to count or add up. The same word sometimes means to suppose or consider.

ecognize   to know something because you have seen it before

record a disc played on a gramophone. The same
word means a written account of something
that has happened and also the best someone
has ever done, like the fastest time for a race.

recorder an instrument you blow into to make
musical sounds

record-player an instrument for playing
gramophone records; the usual word for a
gramophone worked by electricity

recover to find or get something back, which you
have lost. The same word also means to get
better after being ill.

recreation something people like to do in their
spare time, such as sport or gardening

rectangle a shape with four sides
and four right angles

recur to happen again

red a bright colour. Fire engines are usually red.

reduce to make something smaller or less in
quantity

reed a tall stiff grass that grows in or near water.
Reeds are usually hollow.

reef a line of rocks lying just under the water, so
that the waves break over it

reek to smell very strongly and usually
unpleasantly

reel a lively dance. The same word also means a
circular piece of wood or metal on which wire,
thread or string is wound.

refer to mention or speak of: to look up information in a book

referee someone who has to see that rules are obeyed in games and sports

reflect to throw back light or heat from a shiny surface

refreshment a light snack or a drink that makes you feel better when you are tired

refrigerator a cold box or room where food is stored to keep it fresh

refuge a shelter

refuse to say you will not do something you are asked to do

regard to look at. The same word also means to think well or affectionately of someone.

register a written list of names or things kept for a special purpose

regret to feel sorry about something

regular usual; always happening at the same time

rehearse to practise for a performance

reign the period of time that a king or queen rules

reindeer a kind of large deer that lives in very cold places

reins   leather straps used to guide a horse

rejoice   to feel full of joy; very happy

relation   someone who is connected with your family, like a cousin or an aunt

relative   another word for relation

relax   to rest and take it easy

release   to let go; to set free

relent   to become less angry with someone; to forgive

reliable   able to be trusted

relieve   to give help; to reduce a pain or worry. The same word also means to take over work or duty from someone else.

religion   a belief in God or gods

religious   believing in and worshipping God or gods

rely   to trust or depend on

remain   to stay behind or to be left

remainder   the part left over; the rest of

remark   something someone says

remember   to keep something in your mind always or bring something back into your mind; the opposite of forget

remind   to make someone remember something

remove   to take away or take off

rent   the money you pay for the use of something you do not own, such as a house or machine

repair   to mend; to put right

repeat   to say or do over again

repent   to be sorry for something you have said or done; to regret

replace   to put back

reply   to answer

report   to write or tell about something that has happened. The same word also means the noise when a gun is fired.

represent   to speak or act for someone or something else

reproach   to scold or blame someone for what he has done

reptile   a crawling or creeping cold-blooded scaly animal, such as a snake or a crocodile

request   to ask someone to do something; to ask for something

require   to need

rescue   to save, to take someone away from danger

resemble   to look like someone or something else

reservoir   a man-made lake for storing water

resist   to struggle or fight against someone who is trying to make you do something you don't want to do

resolve   to make up your mind; to decide to do something

respect   to admire or have a very good opinion of someone

responsible looking after the safe keeping of someone or something

rest to stop working or playing and be quiet

restaurant a place where you can buy and eat food

result whatever happens at the end of some action. For example, if you go out without your coat you may catch cold as a result.

retreat to go back or run away from danger

return to come back again or give something back

reveal to show something that is hidden or secret

revenge to get your own back on someone who has hurt or injured you

reverse the opposite; the other way

revolution the overthrowing of a government by rebels who want another kind of government

revolt to rebel against authority

revolve to turn around in a circle

revolver a kind of pistol

reward something you get in return for something you have done, such as a prize for winning a race

rhinoceros a large wild animal with a very thick skin and one or two horns on its snout

rhododendron   an evergreen shrub with large leaves and large, beautifully coloured flowers

rhubarb   a plant with thick red stalks that taste good when they are cooked with sugar

rhyme (*say rime*)   words that have the same sound at the end, like *blue*, *zoo* and *shoe*

rhythm (*say rithm*)   a regular pattern or beat of music that you can keep time to

rib   one of the rounded bones between your shoulders and your waist

ribbon   a narrow piece of silky or velvety cloth used to make your hair or your clothes look pretty

rice   the seeds of a food plant that grows in hot countries. Rice grains are hard, but become soft when they are cooked.

rich   having lots of money

rick   a stack or pile of hay

rid   to remove entirely

riddle   a special kind of question. You have to be clever and try to guess the answer.

ride   to be carried on a vehicle or an animal

rider   someone who rides

ridge   a long narrow top of a hill between valleys; a narrow raised strip of something

ridicule   to make fun of or laugh at someone

ridiculous   silly; foolish; laughable

rifle   a long gun

right the opposite of left and the opposite of wrong. The same word also means the correct and proper thing to say or do.

right angle an angle of 90 degrees. The corners of a square are all right angles.

rim the outside edge of something round, like the rim of a wheel

ring a circle. Some rings are made of gold or silver and pretty stones, to be worn on your fingers. The same word also means the sound of a bell.

ring-master a man who announces the acts in a circus

rink a large circle or square of ice that you can skate on

rinse to take soap away by washing in clear water

riot a noisy disturbance by a lot of people, often dangerous and violent

rip to tear something

ripe ready to eat

ripple a small wave or movement on the surface of water

rise to move upwards; to go higher

risk a chance that you may lose something or be harmed in some way

river a large amount of water that flows across the land into a lake or sea

road a hard level surface with no trees or buildings in the way, so that vehicles can get from one place to another

roam   to wander about

roar   a loud deep noise made by big animals like lions and tigers when they are angry

roast   to cook meat in an oven

rob   to take something that is not yours; to steal by force

robber   someone who steals by force

robe   a long garment that covers you down to your ankles

robin   a small wild bird with a red breast and brown and grey feathers

rock   a large piece of stone. The same word also means to move back and forth or from side to side.

rocket   a kind of firework. The same word also means a machine that is shot up into space, sometimes carrying astronauts.

rod   a long thin stick or bar, usually of wood or metal

rogue   a person who is dishonest; a cheat

roll   to move along by turning over and over. The same word also means a kind of bread.

roller   a machine which rolls to move along, or to make things flat and smooth. The same word also means a hair curler.

roller-skates   skates with wheels

rolling-pin   a tube-shaped piece of wood or metal used to flatten dough or pastry before it is cooked

rompers   a child's overall with short trousers pulled together above the knees by elastic

roof   the covering on top of a building or car

rook   a black bird like a crow. It has a hoarse loud cry.

room   a part of the inside of a house such as a bedroom or kitchen

rooster   an adult male chicken; a cock

root   the part of a plant or tree that grows underground

rope   very thick string. It is used to tie heavy things together.

rose   a beautiful sweet-smelling flower with a prickly stem

rosy   pinky-red colour

rot   to go bad or decay

rotten   bad, spoiled. Apples go rotten if they are kept too long.

rough   not smooth; bumpy

round   curved like a circle

roundabout   a machine at the fair which you can ride on as it goes round and round. The same word also means a circle where roads meet.

rouse   to awaken or to stir up somebody's feelings

route (*say root*)   the exact way you go to get from one place to another

rove   to roam or wander about

rover   someone who doesn't stay in one home for very long, but wanders from place to place

row (*rhymes with no*)   a line of things or people. The same word also means to move a boat through water, using oars.

row (*rhymes with now*)   a noisy quarrel or fight

royal   to do with a king or queen

rub   to move something against something else, such as rubbing polish on furniture with a cloth

rubber   a material that stretches or bounces. The same word also means something that takes away pencil marks.

rubbish   something worn out or of no value that you throw away. The same word also means nonsense.

ruby   a jewel, deep red in colour

rudder   a piece of wood or metal at the back of a boat or aeroplane, used for steering

rude   the opposite of polite; bad-mannered. The same word sometimes means rough.

rug   a small floor mat or carpet. The same word also means a kind of blanket used when travelling.

rugged   rough and strong

ruin   to spoil or destroy; to make something useless. The same word also means an old building that is falling down.

rule what you must or must not do. You must obey the rules at school. The same word also means a ruler for measuring.

ruler a straight piece of wood used for measuring things. The same word also means a man or woman who is the head of a country.

rum a strong drink made from sugar cane

rumble a low-pitched, deep rolling sound, like far-away thunder

rumour something said about a person or events that may or may not be true

rumpus a disturbance

run to move quickly on your feet

rung a piece of metal or wood used as a step in a ladder

rural to do with the country; the opposite of urban

rush to hurry; to move quickly to get somewhere on time. The same word also means a tall kind of grass growing near water.

rusk a kind of dry, very crisp toast or biscuit

rust a reddish-brown coating that appears on things made of iron or steel after they have been in water or out in damp air for some time

rustle a soft whispering sound, such as is made by dry leaves rubbing together

rut a deep track made by a wheel in soft ground

rye a kind of grain

sack a large bag made of cloth, paper or plastic

sacred holy

sad not happy; feeling sorry

saddle a leather seat for a rider, which is fastened on to a horse's back or a bicycle

safari an expedition in Africa in search of wild animals

safe not able to hurt you; out of danger. The same word also means a very strong metal box used to lock money and valuable things away safely.

safety freedom from harm or danger

sag to sink down or bend in the middle; to hang limply or droop

saga a long story about people and legends of olden days; a long story about a family and their family before them

sail a piece of canvas fastened to a ship's mast. Sails catch the wind so that the ship is moved along.

sailor a man who works on a ship

saint a very good and holy person

salad a mixture of cold vegetables, such as lettuce, tomatoes and beetroot. Often cold meat, fish or eggs are added to salads, and some salads have fruit in them.

salary money paid regularly, usually every month, for work done

sale the exchange of something for money. The same word also means a period when shops sell some of their goods more cheaply.

saliva the liquid that keeps the inside of your mouth moist

salmon a large fish with silvery scales and pink flesh

salt a white powder we get from the earth and from sea water. It is used in cooking or at meals to make food taste better.

salute to greet someone, usually by raising your right hand to your forehead

same not different; like something else

sample one of, or a small part of something that shows what the rest of it is like

sand small grains of rock which we find in large quantities at the seaside or in the desert

sandal a light shoe, held on the foot by straps

sandwich two pieces of bread with meat or some other food between them

sap the juice in plants and trees

sardine a small fish, usually sold in tins

sari a long piece of cloth wrapped around the body and hanging loose over the shoulder, worn by girls and women in India

sash a strip of ribbon or cloth worn round the waist or over the shoulder. The same word also means the frame of a window that slides up and down.

satchel a bag, used for carrying school books

satellite a planet that revolves around another larger planet, as the moon revolves around the earth

satin a soft shiny material

satisfactory good enough; pleasing

satisfy to do all you can to please someone, or to fill a need

sauce liquid poured over food to give it more flavour. Mint sauce is used with roast lamb.

saucepan a cooking pot with a lid and a handle

saucer a small curved plate put under a cup

saucy cheeky; a bit impudent

sausage a meat mixture chopped up very small and put into a thin bag made of animal skin

savage fierce and cruel; wild

save to keep something to use later on. The same word also means to help someone who is in danger.

saw a metal tool with pointed teeth on one edge, used for cutting wood

sawdust powder from wood that has been sawn

say to speak; to tell something

saying a thing that is often said, like *A stitch in time saves nine.*

scab the dry crust on a sore place or wound when it begins to heal

scabbard a case or holder for a sword; a sheath

scald to burn yourself with a very hot liquid or steam

scale one of the small horny flakes that cover the skin of snakes and fishes. The same word also means a set of notes in music.

scales a weighing machine

scar the mark left on your skin after a sore or wound has healed

scarce not enough; difficult to find

scarcely hardly; not quite

scarcity a very small supply of something, so that there is not enough to go round

scarecrow something, usually like the dummy figure of a man, which is put in a field to frighten the birds away from the crops

scared afraid

scarf a long thick piece of material you wear to keep your neck warm

scarlet bright red

scatter to throw things around in all directions, like scattering bread crumbs on the ground for birds to eat

scene a view: the place where something happens: part of a play

scenery what you see when you look around you, such as hills and fields and trees in the country. The same word also means the painted curtains and other things used on a stage to make it look like a real place.

scent a smell. The same word also means a liquid with a sweet pleasant smell; a perfume.

sceptre a rod or staff, usually of gold or silver, carried by a king or queen at ceremonies

scholar a person who studies; a pupil or student

scholarship knowledge or learning. The same word also means a sum of money given to a student each year because of his good work, so that he can afford to go on studying.

school a place where people go to learn

schooner a large sailing ship

science knowledge got by careful study and testing of things, often to do with nature. Chemistry is a natural science.

scientific to do with science. When you study chemistry you do scientific experiments.

scientist someone who finds out why things happen on earth and in space

scissors a cutting tool like two knives fastened together in the middle

scold to speak crossly to someone about something he has done

scoop a tool shaped like a deep shovel, that is used to dig up earth or sand. Small scoops are used to measure out dry foods, such as sugar, shelled nuts and flour.

scoot to move away quickly

scooter a small two-wheeled vehicle, moved by pushing with one foot or by an engine

scorch to burn slightly; to dry up with heat. Anything that has been scorched turns a yellowy-brown colour.

score the number of points, goals or marks you get in a game or examination

scorn to think that something or someone is not worth bothering about, or no good

scout someone sent to spy on the enemy: a member of the Boy Scouts

scowl to frown

scramble to climb up on rough ground, usually using your hands and feet

scrap a small piece of something. The same word also means to quarrel or fight.

scrape to rub against something with a rough or sharp edge

scratch a mark made with something sharp. The same word also means to scrape with fingernails or claws.

scrawl to write in an untidy way that is not easy to read

scream a very loud high-pitched cry of surprise, pain or fear

screech a piercing scream

screen a light-weight wall that you can move about. The same word also means what a television or cinema picture is shown on.

screw a special kind of thick nail with grooves. You turn it round and round with a tool called a screwdriver to make it go into wood.

scribble   to write in a careless and untidy way

script   handwriting, or printing that looks like handwriting

scrub   to rub something, usually with a brush, to get it clean

scullery   a small room next to the kitchen, where rough kitchen work is done

sculpture   the art of carving stone and wood, or modelling clay or metal into statues and beautiful designs

scurry   to hurry along in a bustling way

sea   the salty water that covers parts of the earth where there is no land

seagull   a sea bird, usually coloured grey and white. It makes a loud screeching sound.

seahorse   a pretty little sea animal with no legs. Its body ends in a curly tail to help it swim along in an upright position.

seal   a fish-eating animal that can also live on land. The same word also means to close or fasten something, so that it cannot be opened without breaking the fastening.

sea lion   a large kind of seal. The male makes a roaring noise, like a lion.

seam   a line where two pieces of material are joined together by sewing

seaplane an aeroplane that can take off from or land on the sea

search to look everywhere for something

searchlight a very powerful beam of light that shows things clearly in the dark

seashell the hard covering on some kinds of fish and sea animals

seaside a place by the sea, where you can go for your holidays

season spring, summer, autumn and winter are the four seasons of the year. The same word also means to add things like salt and pepper to food to improve the flavour.

seat a piece of furniture for sitting on

seaweed plants that grow in the sea

second next after first. The same word also means a measurement of time. There are 60 seconds in a minute.

secondary next after primary; second in importance

secret something known only to you or to a very few other people

secretary someone who writes or types business letters in an office

section a part or a piece of something

secure safe; fastened tightly

see to use your eyes to look at something

seed   the part of the plant from which new plants grow

seek   to look for

see-saw   a strong board fastened in the middle to a heavy piece of wood or metal. Two people can sit on it, one on each end, and go up and down in turn.

seize   to grasp and hold on to

seldom   not often

select   to choose

self   your own person

selfish   thinking only of yourself, and not caring much about other people's wishes

sell   to give something in exchange for money

semi-circle   a half circle

semolina   small hard particles of wheat, usually cooked in a pudding

send   to make a person or thing go somewhere

senior   someone who is older or more important than others

sensation   a feeling

sense   good or right knowledge. The same word also means being able to tell what things are like by tasting, smelling, touching, seeing or hearing.

senseless   foolish; without good sense. The same word also means not to be conscious of what is going on around you.

sensible   wise; having good sense

sentence   a number of words that make a complete thought when put together. The same word also means a punishment for breaking the law.

sentry   a soldier who keeps guard

separate   not joined together; divided

sequin   a small round shiny ornament sewn on clothing to make it sparkle

sergeant   an officer in the army or police

serial   a story or film that appears in parts and not all at one time

series   a number of things or events following one another in regular order

serious   not foolish or making fun; deeply thoughtful. The same word also means causing worry, as when someone has a serious illness.

serpent   another word for snake

servant   someone who is paid to work in someone else's house

serve   to work for someone; to hand out food at meals; to sell things over the counter in a shop

serviette   another word for table napkin

settee   a long seat with a back and arms, with room for several people to sit

settle   to agree upon something, such as settling on a day to go out with someone

several   more than two of something; a few

severe   very serious: not merciful

sew   to join cloth together with a needle and thread

sex   either of the two groups, male and female, that animals and humans are divided into

shabby   nearly worn out; almost ragged. The same word also means not fair or kind, as when someone plays a shabby trick on you.

shade   to keep the light away from something

shadow   a dark shape that appears on the ground when an object gets in the way of light

shaggy   covered with rough long hair or fur, usually untidy

shake   to move something quickly up and down or from side to side

shallow   the opposite of deep; not very far to the bottom

shame   a feeling of unhappiness because you have hurt someone or done something you know is wrong

shameful   wrong; mean

shampoo   to wash your hair

shamrock   a kind of clover plant with tiny leaves divided into three sections

shape   what something is like if you draw a line around the outside of it. A ball is shaped like a circle.

share   to give part of something to someone else

shark   a large dangerous sea fish, which has very sharp teeth

sharp having an edge that can cut or a point that can make holes

shatter to break something into many pieces

shave to cut off hair with a razor

shawl a square piece of cloth folded and worn around the head and shoulders by girls and women

sheaf a bundle (of corn) or a bunch (of papers)

shears large scissors, used for cutting things like hedges or sheep's wool

sheath a scabbard; a cover for the blade of a sword or knife

shed a hut made of wood or metal, often used to keep tools in

sheep an animal covered with thick wool

sheet a large piece of cloth used on a bed. The same word also means a single piece of paper, glass or metal.

shelf a board fastened to a wall. You can keep books and other things on it.

shell the hard covering on a nut or egg. Some fish, animals and insects also have shells.

shelter a place where you are safe from danger or from bad weather

shepherd a man who looks after sheep

sheriff the chief government officer in a county or district

shield something you hide behind or hold up to protect yourself from attack

shift   to move something, usually something heavy. The same word also means a group of people working together for a number of hours, such as a night shift.

shilling   a silver-coloured coin, worth five pence

shimmer   to shine with a soft trembling light

shine   to give out bright light. Silver and gold are shiny; a torch shines in the dark.

shingle   the small rounded stones that are found at the edge of the sea. The same word also means one of the flat pieces of wood used like slates to cover a roof.

ship   a very large boat that goes across the ocean

shipwreck   a ship that has been sunk or destroyed, usually by a storm at sea

shirt   a piece of clothing worn on the upper part of the body by men and boys

shiver   to shake because you are cold

shock   a nasty surprise

shoe   a covering for your foot

shoot   to send a bullet from a gun, or an arrow from a bow

shop   a place where you can buy things

shore   land at the edge of a lake or the sea

short   not very long; not very tall

shorthand   a quick way of writing down what is said

shot   small bullets for a shotgun

shoulder   the joint between your arm and body

shout   to speak or call out very loudly

shove   to push roughly

shovel   a tool like a spade, but wider

show   to point out; to guide. The same word also means a spectacle.

shower   a sudden brief fall of rain, sleet or snow. The same word also means a bath in which you stand up and water sprays all over you.

shred   a scrap or strip torn off something

shriek   a high-pitched scream; a shrill laugh

shrill   high-pitched and piercing to the ears

shrimp   a small grey shellfish that turns pink when cooked

shrink   to become less or smaller. Some kinds of cloth shrink when they have been washed.

shrivel   to dry up and become smaller. A raisin is a shrivelled grape.

shrub   a small woody plant that doesn't grow very tall; a bush

shudder   to shiver or tremble with fear or disgust

shuffle   to move your feet along without lifting them. The same word also means to mix a pack of cards before playing a game.

shunt   to move railway carriages and wagons from one track to another

shut closed, not open

shutter a wooden cover for a window, used to keep heat and light out in daytime, and to keep burglars out at night

shuttlecock a toy made of feathers stuck in a cork, used in the game of badminton

shy not wanting to be with lots of other people

sick ill, not well

sideboard a large, heavy piece of furniture like a cupboard, where dishes, table linen and cutlery are kept

siege an attempt to capture a town or fort by surrounding it, so that help cannot reach it

sieve a container with many small holes, used to separate large and small lumps of soil, grain or food

sift to separate grains or powder from larger lumps by means of a sieve

sigh to breathe out heavily when you are tired or sad

sight the ability to see

sign a movement to show what you mean, like nodding your head to mean *yes*. The same word also means a mark or notice that tells you something, like a traffic sign.

signal a message sent by signs

silent not making a sound

silk very fine smooth cloth made from threads that silkworms spin

silkworm   a caterpillar that spins silk threads

sill   the wooden or stone ledge at the bottom of a door or window

silly   not clever; not thinking carefully

silver   a shiny greyish-white metal. Money, knives, forks and spoons are sometimes made of silver. The same word also means the colour of the metal.

similar   like, or almost like something else

simple   easy, not difficult. The same word also means foolish, not very clever.

since   from a certain time until now, as when you say you have had nothing to eat since breakfast

sincere   honest; meaning what you say

sing   to make music with your voice

singe (*say sinj*)   to burn slightly, to scorch

single   only one. The same word also means not married.

singular   one only, not plural. The same word also means unusual, extraordinary.

sink   a place in the kitchen where there is running water for washing dishes and preparing vegetables. The same word also means to go under the water.

sip   to drink something a little bit at a time

siren   a hooter or whistle that makes a loud, wailing noise

sister   a daughter of the same parents

sit to be on a chair or seat

site an area of ground where a building is, or will be built

situation the place or position of something. The same word also means a job.

size the amount of space something takes up

skate a metal blade or wheels fastened on a shoe, so that you can move quickly and smoothly on ice or a flat surface. The same word also means a large flat fish with very wide fins.

skeleton all the bones inside your body

sketch a rough quick drawing

ski (*say skee*) to move quickly over hard snow on two long pieces of wood called skis, which are fastened to your boots

skid to slide sideways, as a car sometimes does on wet or icy roads

skilful clever; able to do something well

skill cleverness; the ability to do something well

skim to glide quickly over the surface of something. The same word also means to take the cream off the top of the milk.

skin the outside covering of your body

skip to jump up and down on one leg at a time, often over a rope. The same word also means to leave out something, like skipping dull parts of a book.

skipper the captain of a ship

skirt a garment that hangs down from the waist; the part of a dress that hangs down from the waist

skittle one of the nine bottle-shaped pieces of wood in the game of skittles

skull the bony part of your head

skunk a small black animal with white stripes and a bushy tail. It gives out a very bad-smelling liquid when it is in danger.

sky the air above you that you see when you look up out of doors

skylark a lark, a small bird which sings when it is flying very high up in the air

skyscraper a very tall building

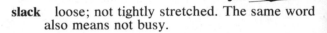

slab a thick slice

slack loose; not tightly stretched. The same word also means not busy.

slam to shut or bang something with a loud noise

slanting not straight up and down; sloping, like this line /

slap to hit with the palm of the hand

slash to make long cuts in something, sometimes violently

slate   a kind of stone used for roofs

slaughter   killing of animals, usually for food: a terrible killing of one person or great numbers of people

slave   someone who is not free because he is owned by another person and has to work for him

slay   to kill

sled   a vehicle with metal or wooden runners, that moves easily over snow-covered ground

sledge   a sled

sleek   smooth and shiny, like the coat of a horse which has been well fed and cared for

sleep   You sleep when you are not awake.

sleet   rain mixed with snow or hail

sleeve   the part of your clothes that covers your arm

sleeveless   without sleeves

sleigh   a large sled, usually pulled by horses

slender   slim; narrow; not looking strong or heavy

slice   a flat piece cut from something, like a slice of bread or cake

slide   to move smoothly down or along on something

slight   small in quantity or importance; slim or slender

slightly   by a small amount

slim   thin; narrow; not fat

slime   thin slippery mud or dirt

sling   a piece of leather used for throwing stones: a piece of cloth tied around your neck and shoulder to hold up a broken or injured arm

slip   to slide when you don't mean to. The same word also means to move away quickly and quietly.

slipper   a soft shoe you wear indoors

slippery   smooth on the surface so that you slip in walking, as on ice or thin mud

slit   a long thin cut

slop   to spill

slope   ground that goes upwards or downwards; slanting; not straight

slot   a narrow opening, usually in a machine, for something like a coin to fit in

slouch   to walk or move in a lazy droopy way, not holding yourself up straight

slow   the opposite of fast. To be slow is to take a long time to do something.

sludge   nasty soft mud

slug   a large kind of snail without a shell

slush   melting snow; soft mud

sly   cunning; artful

smack   to hit with the open hand; to slap

small   another word for little; the opposite of large

smart   clever; quick to learn: well dressed, stylish

smash   to break something into pieces, usually with a crashing noise

smear   to spread or rub something greasy or sticky so as to leave a dirty mark

smell   what your nose tells you about something

smile   to look happy

smith   a man who makes things out of metal, like a silversmith or blacksmith

smock   a loose garment, usually worn over other clothes to keep them clean

smoke   the cloud of tiny particles that comes from something burning

smooth   without any bumps; the opposite of rough

smother   to cover completely: to stop someone breathing by covering his mouth and nose

smoulder   to burn slowly without much flame

smudge   a stain, a smear of dirt

smuggle   to bring something secretly into one country from another without paying tax

snack   a small quick meal, like a sandwich or biscuits and cheese

snail   a small animal that moves very slowly. It has a shell on its back.

snake   a crawling animal with a long body and no legs. Some snakes are dangerous because they have a poisonous bite.

snap   to break with a sudden sharp noise. The same word also means a card game for children.

snarl   to make a growling noise, with the teeth showing. The same word also means a knot or tangle.

snatch   to grab something quickly

sneak   to tell tales about someone behind his back: to creep along quietly

sneer   to smile in a scornful or mocking way

sneeze   to make a sudden blowing noise through your nose because it tickles

sniff   to take in a noisy breath through your nose

snip   to cut a little piece off something, usually with scissors

snooker   a game played with coloured balls on a special table

snore   to make a loud breathing noise through your mouth when you are asleep

snorkel   a tube with one end sticking out of the water so that swimmers can stay under and still keep breathing air

snout   the sticking-out nose and mouth of some animals such as pigs and porpoises

snow   drops of water that become frozen in the air in winter. The pieces that float down through the air are called snowflakes.

snowball   a ball of snow pressed together

snowdrop   a little white flower which appears in very early spring

snowman   a man made out of snow

snowshoe   one of a pair of frames strung with thin strips of leather. People wear snowshoes to keep their feet from sinking into deep soft snow.

snug   cosy and warm

soak   to make something or someone very wet

soap   something you use with water to make things clean

soar   to fly high into the air

sob   to weep noisily

sock   something you put on to cover your feet and ankles before you put on your shoes

socket   a hollow place that you fit something into, like a socket for an electric bulb

sofa   another word for couch

soft   not hard, rough or loud

soggy   damp and heavy; very wet

soil   loose earth. The same word also means to make something dirty.

solar   having to do with the sun

soldier   a man in the army

sole   the bottom of your foot or your shoe. The same word also means a kind of flat fish.

solemn   serious; very earnest

solid   hard and firm all through, not hollow or liquid

solitary   alone; by yourself

solve   to find the answer to something puzzling or difficult

some   a few; not all

somebody   a person who is not named

someone   another word for somebody

somersault   to go head over heels

sometime   at a time not known

sometimes   not all the time; now and then

something   a thing not named

somewhat   rather; a little

somewhere   at an unknown place

son   a male child of a father or mother

song   words and music together, which you sing. The same word also means the musical notes sung by birds.

sonic   having to do with sound waves, as in sonic boom

soon   in a short time

soot   a soft black powdery stuff which comes from burning wood or coal. It sticks to the inside of the chimney.

soothe   to calm someone down; to comfort

sore   painful when touched

sorrow   unhappiness; sadness

sorry   feeling unhappy about something you have done, or something that has happened

sort   to put together things that belong together

soul   the invisible part of a person which is believed to live on after death

sound   anything that can be heard

soup   a liquid food made by boiling meat, vegetables or other foods together in water

sour   not sweet tasting. Lemons taste sour.

source   the beginning or starting place of something, like a stream or river

south   the direction opposite to north, on your right as you face the rising sun

sou'wester   a waterproof hat which covers the back of the neck. The same word also means a wind blowing from the south-west.

sow (*rhymes with no*)   to scatter seed over the ground or plant it in the ground

sow (*rhymes with now*)   a female pig

space   a place with nothing in it. The same word is often used to mean the sky higher than aeroplanes can fly, where there is not even any air.

spaceship   a special machine moved by rocket motors that can go far up into space to the moon and beyond

spade a tool used for digging in the ground

spaghetti long tubes of dried wheat paste, like macaroni only much longer and thinner

span the distance between the tip of your thumb and little finger when your hand is stretched out. The same word also means the length of anything from end to end.

spangle a thin piece of shiny metal sewn on to a garment. Lots of spangles sewn on to a dress make it glitter and sparkle.

spaniel a kind of dog with a silky coat and long floppy ears

spank to smack with your open hand

spanner a tool for tightening or loosening nuts and bolts

spare to let something go. The same word also means extra. If you have two copies of the same book, one of them is a spare copy.

spark a tiny bit of something burning, that flies out of the fire

sparkle to give off bright flashes of light; to glitter. Snow sparkles in the sunlight.

sparkler a firework which gives off silver or coloured sparks when you light it

sparrow a small brown and grey bird

speak to say something

spear a pole with a metal point on the end. It is used as a weapon.

special not like anything else; made for one use only

specimen   one of something; a sample

speck   a small spot or dirty mark; a tiny piece

speckled   marked with lots of small spots

spectacle   something interesting which makes people
   want to look at it

spectacles   another word for the glasses people wear
   to help them to see better

spectator   someone who looks on or watches others
   doing something

speech   the act of speaking. The same word also
   means a talk or lecture.

speed   quickness, swiftness

spell   to put letters together in the right order to
   make up a certain word. The same word also
   means magic words which are supposed to
   make something happen.

spend   to pay out money

spice   dried or powdered flavourings for food,
   usually tasting and smelling strongly

spider   a small animal with eight legs. It spins a web
   to catch insects.

spike   a long sharp point. The same word also
   means an ear of grain or a tall cluster of
   flowers on a stem.

spill   to let something, such as powder or liquid
   accidentally run out from a container

spin   to go round and round. The same word also
   means to make thread out of raw wool, cotton
   or flax.

spinach a dark green leafy vegetable

spindle a thin rod on which thread is twisted in spinning

spine the backbone of a person or animal. The same word also means a thorn, or one of the thin, stiff prickles growing on some animals, such as hedgehogs.

spinster an unmarried woman

spiral something that winds upwards, going round and round in continuous curves

spire the long pointed top of a church steeple

spirit another word for soul; a ghost

spit to throw out something from your mouth

spite a wish to be cruel to someone or to hurt his feelings

spiteful saying and doing cruel things to someone you don't like

splash the noise of something heavy falling into liquid. The same word also means to throw liquid about.

splashdown the landing of a space capsule in the ocean

splendid wonderful; very rich and grand; very good

splinter a tiny thin piece of wood, glass or metal, which has broken off from a larger piece

split to break or cut something from end to end

spoil to damage something or make it of no use. The same word also means to give a child his own way too much.

sponge   the soft, yellowish skeleton of a sea animal, which becomes much softer when it soaks up water. It is used for washing yourself. The same word also means a kind of soft cake.

spool   a reel on which you wind things like thread, ribbon, or film

spoon   a tool used in cooking and eating food

sport   a game, usually played outdoors. Football and cricket are sports.

spot   a small mark

spout   a small tube or pipe through which liquid is poured, like the spout of a teapot

sprain   to twist a joint or muscle so badly that it swells

sprawl   to sit or lie in a relaxed position, with your arms and legs spread out

spray   to send out fine drops of liquid

spread   to cover a surface, like spreading butter on bread

spring   to move quickly and suddenly. The same word also means a piece of metal which can be pressed down but jumps back into position when you let it go. The word also means the season after winter, when plants begin to grow.

sprinkle   to scatter small drops of water or bits of something, like sugar or sawdust

sprout   to begin to grow. The same word also means a green vegetable like a tiny cabbage. Its full name is a brussels sprout.

spurt   to squirt out suddenly; a rush of liquid

spy someone who secretly watches what other people are doing, especially during a war when he is paid to get information about the enemy

square a rectangle whose four sides are equal in length

squash to crush or squeeze something out of shape. The same word also means a bottled drink made of fruit, sugar and water.

squaw an American Indian woman

squeak a small high sound. A mouse squeaks and so does a rusty door hinge.

squeal a long high piercing sound made by some animals

squeeze to press hard; to crush; to hug

squirrel a small red or grey animal with a long bushy tail

squirt to force liquid out of an opening in a sudden stream; to spurt

stab to pierce or cut with a pointed weapon

stable a building where horses are kept

stack a large heap

stadium an open-air sports ground with rows of seats all round

staff a group of people working together, like people in an office, or teachers in a school. The same word also means a pole or stick carried in the hand.

stag   a male deer

stage   the platform in a theatre or hall where people act, sing, or speak

stage coach   a horse-drawn coach which travelled across the country in olden days, stopping at certain places to let people off or on

stagger   to walk unsteadily, lurching and stumbling

stain   a dirty mark

staircase   a number of stairs, usually with a side-rail to keep you from falling

stairs   a set of steps in a building for walking up or down

stake   a strong pointed stick or post

stale   not fresh; dry and without much taste because of being kept too long

stalk   another word for stem. The same word also means to creep quietly after an animal that you are hunting.

stall   a kind of table on which things for sale are shown at a market. The same word also means a place for one animal in a cattle shed or stable.

stallion   a male horse

stammer   to repeat the beginning of a word several times before going on to say the whole word; to speak in jerks and pauses

stamp a little piece of coloured paper you stick on a letter or parcel, which pays for sending it by post. The same word also means to hit the floor hard with the sole of your foot.

stand to be on your feet; not sitting. The same word also means rows of raised seats for people watching an outdoor game.

standard a flag. The same word also means a grade.

star a tiny light which shines in the night sky. The same word also means someone who is famous and popular, like a film star.

stare to look at something or someone for a long time without looking away

starfish a flat sea animal with five arms like the points of a star

starling a wild bird with glossy, dark greenish-purple feathers, speckled with white

start to begin: to move suddenly

startle to make a person or animal start with sudden fear or surprise

starvation suffering or death caused by lack of food

starve to be in great need of food; to die of hunger

statement something said or told

station the place where a train stops to let people on or off. The same word also means a building for policemen or firemen.

stationary not moving; standing still

stationery writing paper and envelopes

statue the figure of a person or animal which is carved from stone or wood. Sometimes statues are made of metal or some other material.

stay to be in one place and not leave

steadily in a steady, firm way

steady standing firm; moving without jerking or shaking. The same word also means loyal and faithful.

steak a thick slice of meat or fish

steal to take something which belongs to someone else

steam the cloud-like gas that water turns into when it boils

steel a very strong metal made from iron

steep rising nearly straight up from the ground, like a steep hill

steeple a high pointed tower on a church

steer to guide a vehicle or ship to the right or left. The same word also means a young bull.

stellar having to do with the stars

stem the thin part of a plant that holds up the flowers or leaves

step to put one foot in front of the other when walking. The same word also means one stair in a staircase.

stern severe; strict; grim. The same word also means the back part of a ship or boat.

stew to cook food, especially meat with vegetables, by boiling it slowly

stick a long thin piece of wood: anything shaped like a stick, such as a stick of wax or gum

stickleback a small river-fish with prickles or spines on its back

sticky clinging or holding on, as when something like glue or honey sticks to your fingers

stiff firm; hard; not easily bent or moved

stile a little set of steps fixed to a fence or a wall to help you climb over

still not moving; calm

stilt one of a pair of tall poles with foot rests

sting the sharp part of an insect, like a pin, which can hurt you

stir to move; to shake up or mix

stirrup a metal ring hanging down each side of a saddle. It is flat at the bottom so that you can put your foot in it when you ride a horse.

stitch a loop of thread that has been sewn. The same word also means a sudden sharp pain in your side, usually caused by running.

stock supplies of food and other goods stored by shop-keepers. The same word also means a sweet-smelling garden flower.

stocking a kind of sock that covers the whole of your leg. Stockings are usually made of nylon, wool or silk.

stoke to put fuel on the fire to make it hotter

stole a long, narrow piece of material, often made of fur or silk, worn over the shoulders and hanging down

stomach a kind of pocket in the middle of your body, which holds food after it has been swallowed

stone a small piece of rock. The same word also means the hard seed inside some fruit like plums and cherries.

stool a little seat with no back or arms

stoop to bend the upper part of your body downwards

stop to end or leave off what you are doing

stopper something you put in the neck of a bottle to close the opening

store to keep something until it is needed. The same word also means a shop.

stork a large bird with very long legs and a long beak

storm a sudden outburst of bad weather with heavy rain, snow or hail, and sometimes thunder and lightning

story an adventure told or written. It can be a true story, or made up like a fairy tale.

stove something which makes heat for us to cook food or warm the room

straight not crooked or curved. This is a straight line _____

straighten   to make straight; to put things neat and tidy

strain   to make every effort; to put all your strength into doing something

strainer   a kind of bowl with holes in it, usually made of metal or plastic. You put vegetables or other food in it to let the water out.

strange   unusual; out of place

stranger   someone you do not know

strangle   to kill a person or animal by squeezing its throat; to choke

strap   a long thin piece of leather, usually with a buckle, to fasten something

straw   dry stiff yellow stalks that farm animals like to sleep on

strawberry   a small soft red fruit with a lot of seeds

stray   to wander away or go in the wrong direction by mistake

streak   a stripe or long narrow mark

stream   a small river

streamer   a long thin flag, or a paper decoration for parties

street   a road with houses or other buildings on both sides of it

strength   how strong or powerful something is

stretch   to make longer or wider by pulling

strict   insisting on complete obedience without exception; severe; stern

stride   to walk with long steps

strike   to hit someone or something as hard as you can. The same word also means to stop work because the workers want more money or because they think something at work needs putting right.

string   a long piece of thick thread for tying up things: one of the parts of a musical instrument, such as a violin or guitar

strip   a long narrow piece of something. The same word also means to take off all your clothes.

stripe   a long narrow line or mark of colour, usually in material. Flags often have different coloured stripes on them.

stroke   to rub gently, as you would stroke a cat. The same word also means a blow, or the sound of a clock striking.

stroll   to walk slowly, in no hurry to get anywhere

strong   not weak or easily broken: able to lift heavy things

structure   something constructed, like a dam or a building: the way things are built up or arranged

struggle   to make a great effort; to fight to get free

stubborn   not willing to give way to others; obstinate

stud   a kind of fastening for a shirt

student   someone who studies, usually at a college or university

studio   the workshop of an artist: a place where films are made: a room from which radio or television programmes are broadcast

study to learn; to examine something closely

stuff the material something is made of. The same word also means to pack tightly.

stuffy without enough fresh air

stumble to trip over something or lose your footing

stump the part of a tree trunk that is left after the tree has been cut down

stun to knock someone senseless; to amaze or surprise greatly

stupid foolish; silly; slow to think

sturdy strong; healthy

stutter to speak with difficulty because you find it hard to get words out easily; to stammer

sty a place where pigs are kept. The same word also means a small swelling on the eyelid, often spelled stye.

style the way something is done, such as old-style dancing, the newest style of clothes, or good style in writing

subject a person who is ruled by the head of a country. The same word also means what is being talked or written about—for example, *The subject of the talk was sport.*

submarine a special kind of ship that can go along under water

substance anything solid that you can handle or feel: the main part of something

subtract to take away a number or a quantity from a larger number or quantity

subway an underground passage for pedestrians: an underground electric train

succeed to do what you set out to do. The same word also means to come after, or to follow in order, as when a prince becomes king by succeeding his father.

success a satisfactory ending to something you set out to do, like success in passing an examination or winning a race

suck to draw liquid into your mouth; to keep something in your mouth without chewing it

sudden happening all at once

suddenly unexpectedly; all at once

suds soapy bubbles

suede a soft leather which doesn't shine

suet a kind of hard fat taken from sheep and cattle and used in cooking

suffer to feel pain; to put up with

sufficient enough

sugar a white substance used in food and drinks to make them taste sweet

sugar cane a plant with sweet-tasting stems from which sugar is made

suggest to tell others about an idea or plan that you think would be good

suit a set of clothes, such as a coat and trousers, which are meant to be worn together

suitable   fitting in well; proper; right

suitcase   a flat case for carrying clothes when you are going away

suite   a set of rooms at an hotel or large house. The same word also means a set of furniture for a room.

sulk   to show you are angry and bad-tempered by not speaking and not being friendly

sultana   a small light-coloured raisin

sum   the total number when two or more things are added together

summarize   to go over the main points of what you have been saying or writing

summer   the warmest season of the year, between spring and autumn

summit   the highest point of something, such as the summit of a mountain

sun   the round bright ball seen in the sky during the day. It sends out light and heat.

sunburn   burning or reddening of the skin when you have been too long in the hot sun

sundial   an instrument that shows the time of day by the position of the sun's shadow on a dial

sunny   full of sunshine

sunrise   the time when the sun comes up: the actual rising of the sun

sunset   the time when the sun goes down: the actual setting of the sun

sunshine   the light from the sun

sup   to eat supper: to take spoonfuls of soup or liquid into your mouth

supermarket   a large shop where you can buy all kinds of food and some other things as well. You help yourself and pay when you go out.

supersonic   moving faster than sound travels in air

supper   the last meal before you go to bed

supply   to provide; to give something that is needed

support   to hold something up; to bear the weight of something

suppose   to imagine; to pretend

sure   knowing you are right

surely   without question or doubt

surface   the outside of anything; the top of a lake or the sea or the earth

surgeon   a doctor who cures patients by cutting out or repairing diseased parts of the body

surgery   a doctor's office where you can visit him. The same word also means curing illness by cutting out or repairing the diseased part.

surly   bad-tempered; not friendly

surname   your last name; the family name

surprise   something you don't expect

surrender   to give up

surround   to be all around; on all sides of something

survey   to take a careful look over something or some place

suspect to have a feeling in your mind that something is wrong or that someone is not telling the truth

swallow to let food or drink go down your throat. The same word also means a pretty dark blue and white bird with a forked tail.

swamp wet, marshy ground. The same word also means to put too much water in something.

swan a large water-bird with a very long neck. It is usually white.

swarm a large number of insects, animals or people moving together

sway to swing or move from side to side

swear to make a very solemn promise. The same word also means to use bad language.

sweat the moisture that comes from your skin when you are hot

sweater a heavy knitted jersey

sweep to use a brush or broom to clean the floor. The same word also means a man who sweeps chimneys.

sweet tasting of sugar; not sour

sweetheart someone you love and hope to marry

swell to grow larger or louder

swerve to turn aside quickly, as when you swerve so as not to bump into something when you are running

swift   fast; quick; rapid. The same word also means a bird with long pointed wings that can fly very fast.

swill   to drink in large amounts. The same word also means pigs' food.

swim   to move along in the water using your arms and legs

swing   a seat hanging from ropes or chains. The same word also means to move in the air, back and forth, or from side to side.

swipe   to hit hard and rather wildly

swirl   to move about quickly with a circling movement, as when dried leaves are blown about by the wind

switch   a little lever which turns on electricity

swollen   made bigger by swelling

swop   to exchange something for something else

sword   a very long knife with a special handle, used for fighting or for carrying in some ceremonies

syllable   a group of sounds that make a word or part of a word. The words *boy* and *girl* each have one syllable, the words *women* and *children* have two syllables.

sympathy   a feeling of kindness and pity towards someone who is sad or ill

syrup   a thick sweet liquid made by boiling sugar with water or fruit juice

system   a group of things working together

tab   a small flap or loop, usually on a piece of clothing

table   a piece of furniture with legs and a flat top. The same word also means a set of facts or figures arranged in columns.

tablecloth   a large piece of material used to cover a table

tablet   a small, flat piece of something, like stone, soap and some kinds of medicine

tack   a short nail with a wide flat head. The same word also means to sew something together with long loose stitches.

tackle   to use all your strength to try to do something. The same word also means the equipment for doing something, such as fishing tackle.

tadpole   a frog when it is very young, before its legs develop

taffeta   a kind of stiff shiny cloth used for making dresses

tag   a label. The same word also means a children's game in which one person chases and tries to touch another.

tail   the part that comes out at the end of anything, like the tail of an animal, a kite or an aeroplane

tailor   a man who makes clothes, such as suits, overcoats, skirts and trousers

take   to get hold of: to carry away

tale   another word for a story

talk   to speak or say something

talkative   fond of talking, talking too much

tall very high

tambourine a small thin drum which you tap with your hand. It has small metal discs around the edge which make a tinkling sound when you shake it.

tame not wild; able to live with human beings as pets, like tame rabbits

tamper to meddle or interfere with something

tan the brown colour of your skin when you have been out in the sun for a long time. The same word also means to make animal hide into leather.

tangerine a kind of small sweet orange with a loose skin that comes off easily

tangled all twisted up in knots, like hair that has not been combed

tank a special heavy car made of iron and steel, with big guns in it. The same word also means a large metal or glass container for water and other liquids.

tanker a ship that carries oil or other liquids

tap to hit something lightly. The same word also means a kind of handle that you turn off and on to control the flow of something from a pipe, like gas and water.

tape a narrow strip of something such as strong cloth, plastic or sticky paper used to tie or fasten things together

tape recorder a machine that takes down and plays back sounds on a special kind of tape

tar a thick sticky black liquid which comes from wood and coal. Tar is used in making roads.

tardy late; slow

target something you aim at in shooting

tarmac a kind of surface found on most roads, made with tar. The word is short for tarmacadam.

tart a piece of pastry with jam or fruit in it

tartan a woollen material, especially worn in Scotland. It has a coloured check pattern, and some Scottish families have their own special colours and patterns.

task a job; an amount of work that you have to do

tassel a number of threads all tied in a knot at the top. Tassels are used to decorate clothing or furniture.

taste to put a bit of food in your mouth or sip a drink to see if you like it or not

tax money paid to the government to help them pay for things everyone uses, such as roads, bridges, schools, hospitals and medicine

taxi a car that you pay to ride in

tea a hot drink made by pouring boiling water on to the dried leaves of the tea plant

teach to show someone how to do something; to give lessons

tea cosy a warm cover which you put over a teapot to keep the tea hot

teacher someone who helps you to learn things

team a group of people all helping each other in a job or game

teapot a special pot to make tea in. It has a handle and a spout.

tear (*rhymes with spare*) to pull apart; to rip

tear (*rhymes with spear*) one of the drops of water that come from your eyes when you are sad or hurt

tease to annoy someone by making fun of him

teaser a tricky question or problem

tea set cups and saucers, plates and a teapot which all have the same pattern

teem to be abundant; to be full to overflowing as when a river teems with fish

teeth more than one tooth

telegram a short message which you give to the post office to send by telegraph

telegraph a way to send messages quickly by electricity

telephone an instrument that carries your voice through electric wires so that you can speak to someone far away

telescope an instrument like a tube that you look through to see things that are far away, like the stars

television   an instrument that brings pictures and sound through the air from far away

tell   to give news or say what you know about something

temper   the mood you are in. You can be in a bad temper and be cross with everyone, or in a good temper when you are nice to be with.

temperature   how hot or cold something is. It is measured in degrees.

tempest   a violent storm with a very strong wind

temple   a building in which people pray and worship

tempo   how fast or slow a piece of music has to be played

tempt   to try to persuade someone to do something which he ought not to do

tender   soft; delicate. The same word also means gentle and loving.

tennis   a game played by two or four people. They use rackets to hit a ball back and forth over a net.

tent   a shelter made of a thick piece of cloth held up by strong sticks. You can camp out of doors under it.

tepee   a cone-shaped tent American Indians lived in

tepid   lukewarm

term   a length of time. The school year is divided into three terms, with holidays between.

terminus   the place where buses, trains or aeroplanes end their journeys

terrace a raised flat area of earth: a row of houses joined together

terrible dreadful, awful

terrier a kind of small dog

terrific fearful, alarming. The same word can also be used to mean very great.

terrify to frighten someone very greatly

terror very great fear

test an examination to find out how much someone knows. The same word also means to find out whether something such as a car or a machine is working properly.

tether to tie an animal with a rope or chain so that it can walk around a bit, but cannot get away

thankful grateful; pleased

thank you You say *thank you* when someone has been kind or has given you something, and you want to show him you are pleased.

thatch a roof or covering of straw or reeds

theatre a building where plays are acted

theft the act of stealing

themselves those people; they and no one else

therefore for that reason

thermometer an instrument for measuring how hot or cold something is

thick wide or deep; the opposite of thin

thicket shrubs and trees growing closely together

thief   someone who steals

thigh   the thick part of your leg above the knee

thimble   a metal or plastic cover for the top of your finger. It keeps the needle from hurting you when you are sewing.

thin   not wide or fat; the opposite of thick

thing   an object which is not named

think   to use your mind to help you do things better: to have ideas

third   next after second; one of three

thirsty   wanting to drink

thistle   a plant with a prickly stem and leaves. It grows wild and usually has purple flowers.

thorn   a sharp woody spike or prickle on a bush or shrub

thorough   complete; very careful

thou   an old-fashioned word for *you*

though   although

thought   an idea; something that is in your mind

thoughtful   thinking deeply: thinking of what others would like

thrash   to beat

thread a very thin, very long piece of material used in sewing

threaten to warn someone that you are going to punish or harm him

three-wheeler a vehicle that runs on three wheels

thresh to beat out grain from its covering. Sometimes the word is spelled thrash.

thrill a feeling of excitement

throat the inside of the front of your neck which contains the gullet and the windpipe

throb to quiver; to feel your heart beating strongly, as when you have been running very fast

throne a special chair for a king or queen on ceremonial occasions

throttle to choke or strangle. The same word also means the fuel control of a car engine.

through from one end to the other

throughout in every part

throw to release something like a ball or a stone out of your hand and into the air with some force

thrush a wild song bird with a brown and white speckled breast

thrust to push with great force; to stab

thud a heavy bumping sound when something falls to the ground

thumb   the short thick finger on your hand

thump   to hit with a heavy blow, usually using your fist

thunder   the loud noise which you hear during a storm after a flash of lightning

thus   therefore; in this way

tick   a soft clicking noise such as a clock makes. The same word also means a mark to show that something is correct, like this ✓

ticket   a small piece of paper or cardboard which you get when you pay to ride on a public vehicle, or go to a show

tickle   a funny feeling on your skin which makes you want to scratch. Sometimes it can make you laugh when someone tickles you.

tide   the coming in and going out of the sea

tidy   neat; in order; not in a mess

tie   to make a knot with string or ribbon. The same word also means a narrow piece of cloth worn around the neck.

tiger   a dangerous wild animal like a very large cat. It has a striped fur, and lives mostly in India.

tight   close-fitting; closely packed; the opposite of loose

tighten   to make something tight or tighter

tile a flattish piece of baked clay which is used for roofs and sometimes for floors

till up to a certain time. The same word also means a special drawer where a shopkeeper keeps his money.

tilt to lean to one side

timber wood which is going to be made into something or used for building

time seconds, minutes, hours, days, weeks, months and years

timid easily frightened; the opposite of brave

tin a silvery metal. The same word also means a container made of tin.

tingle a prickly feeling

tinker a man who mends pots and pans

tinkle a small ringing sound

tinsel long strips of silvery sparkling material which are used to decorate Christmas trees

tiny very, very small

tip the thin end of something, usually pointed. The same word also means to overturn or tilt something.

tiptoe to walk on the tips of your toes very quietly

tire to become tired; to bore or make someone tired

tired When you are tired you have the feeling that you want to rest or go to sleep.

tit a small prettily-coloured wild bird

title the name of something, such as a book, a song or a play. The same word also means a word in front of someone's name such as Sir, Lord, Doctor, or Captain.

toad an animal that looks like a frog which has a rough, lumpy skin. It usually lives on land.

toadstool a poisonous plant shaped like a mushroom

toast bread which is made brown and crisp by heating it

tobacco a plant with large leaves which are dried, cut up and used for smoking in cigarettes, cigars or a pipe

toboggan a long flat sledge, curved up at the front, usually without runners

today on this day

toddle to walk with short wobbly steps like a very young child

toe a part of your foot. You have five toes on each foot.

toffee a sweet sticky food made from sugar and butter

together being with

toil to work very hard, with great effort

toilet washing, dressing and doing your hair. The same word also means a lavatory.

tomato a soft round red fruit, often used as a vegetable or in salads

tomb a place where someone is buried, either in the ground or in a stone box above the ground

tomboy a girl who behaves like a boy and enjoys playing boys' games

tomorrow the day after today

ton a measurement of weight. One ton is equal to 2,240 pounds.

tone a sound, usually musical. The word is also used to describe the way a person's voice sounds, such as a harsh or a sweet tone of voice.

tongue the thick soft part inside your mouth that moves when you talk and with which you taste things

tongs a tool with two pieces of metal like pincers for holding and lifting things

tonight this night

tonsil one of two little round pieces of flesh at the back of your mouth. Sometimes they have to be taken out if they become unhealthy.

too as well; also

tool any instrument that helps people to do work. Hammers and shovels are tools.

tooth one of the white bones in your mouth that you use to bite with

toothache a pain in your teeth

toothbrush a small long-handled brush which you use to clean your teeth

toothpaste a paste which you squeeze from a tube on to a toothbrush and use to clean your teeth

top the highest part of something. The same word also means a spinning toy.

topic any subject people choose to speak, write or argue about

torch a light which you can carry about, like an electric torch or a stick which is flaming at one end

torpedo a long rounded bomb which is fired through or along the surface of water

torrent a very fast-moving stream or river

tortoise a slow-moving animal with a very thick shell

torture to make someone suffer great pain, usually to make him confess or admit something

toss to throw something carelessly into the air

tot a small child. The same word also means to add up.

total the sum of; the whole amount

totter to walk unsteadily and shakily

touch to feel something with your fingers or with some part of your body

tough hard; strong; not easily broken

tour to travel round for pleasure from place to place, ending up where you started from

tournament a sports competition which several teams try to win, to see which is the best

tow (*rhymes with go*)   to pull something along by a rope

towards   in the direction of

towel   a piece of thick cloth or paper that you use to dry things that are wet

tower   a building or part of a building that is very high and narrow

town   a lot of houses and buildings together. It is larger than a village.

toy   something children play with

trace   to copy a drawing by putting transparent paper over it and going over the lines with a pencil

track   a rough path through woods or fields. The same word means a railway line.

tractor   a heavy motor with wheels that pulls something along

trade   to buy and sell: to exchange. The same word also means a particular kind of business, like hairdressing or dressmaking.

traffic   cars, buses and vans moving along the streets

tragedy   a disaster; a terribly sad happening

trail   footprints or other signs that have been left by something or someone moving ahead of you

trailer   any wheeled vehicle drawn behind a motor car or lorry

train   a lot of carriages pulled along a railway by an engine. The same word also means to teach.

trainer someone who teaches a person or animal to do something well, like swimming or running in a race

traitor someone who betrays his friends or country

tram a kind of bus which runs on rails and works by electricity

tramp to walk heavily. The same word also means a person who wanders from place to place, often sleeping out of doors and begging for money from other people.

trample to tread heavily on something

trampoline a large piece of canvas fastened to a frame with springs. You can bounce up and down and do somersaults on it.

transfer to carry or send something or someone from one place to another

transform to change the way something looks, as a caterpillar is transformed into a butterfly

translate to express the meaning of words in one language in another language

transparent easily seen through. Window glass is transparent.

transplant to remove a plant from the ground and plant it somewhere else. The same word also means a kind of surgery in which a diseased part of the body is removed and a healthy part put in its place.

transport to carry something from one place to another

trap a way of catching animals or birds

trapdoor a door in the floor or ceiling

trapeze a kind of swing with only a thin bar for a seat

travel to make a journey; to go from place to place

trawler a special fishing boat that drags a large net along the bottom of the sea

tray a flat piece of wood, metal or plastic, on which you can carry light things, such as cups and saucers and food

treacherous not to be trusted; likely to betray

treacle a thick dark sticky food which comes from sugar cane

tread to step or walk

treasure a collection of money or jewels. The same word also means anything which is valuable or much loved.

treat to act in a certain way towards someone or something. The same word also means a special outing or present for which you do not have to pay.

tree a very large plant with leaves and branches

tremble to shake or shiver

tremendous very large; enormous; huge

trench a deep ditch

trespass to go on someone else's land or property without permission

trial a test to see if something works well: the judging of a person in a court of law

triangle   an area with three straight sides

tribe   a group of families who all live together with one chief who rules them

trick   something clever. Some people can do magic tricks and others can do tricks like walking on a wire, or standing on a horse when it is running.

trickle   to flow in a very small stream

tricycle   a three-wheeled cycle

trifle   something small and unimportant. The same word also means a sweet food made of sponge cake, cream or custard, and jelly.

trigger   the little lever which is pulled to fire a gun

trim   to make something neat, often by cutting off rough edges and loose threads. The same word also means to decorate a piece of clothing by adding lace, ribbons or some other pretty trimming.

trip   a short journey. The same word also means to stumble or fall as a result of catching your foot on something.

trolley   a set of trays on wheels; a small hand-cart

trot   to run, but not as fast as you can

trouble   anything which annoys or causes worry or unhappiness

troublesome   causing trouble or difficulty

trough   a long narrow container which holds water or food for animals

trousers a piece of clothing which covers you from your waist to your ankles, fitting around each leg separately

trout a kind of fish which lives in fresh water and is very good to eat

trowel a little spade with a curved blade. It is used in the garden for turning over earth and digging up small plants.

truck a big open vehicle for carrying heavy things from place to place

trudge to walk along wearily, with heavy footsteps

true real; correct

trumpet a musical instrument that you blow into

trunk the thick stem of a tree. The same word also means an elephant's nose, or a big box for sending clothes in.

trust to believe that someone is honest, or that you will not be tricked

truth whatever is true and has really happened

try to test to see if something works: to do the best you can

trying annoying; rather naughty

tub an open container for washing in or for holding liquids

tube a long thin hollow piece of metal, wood or other material. The same word also means a container from which you squeeze out the contents, such as toothpaste. Tube is also another word for an underground railway.

tuck to roll or fold up. The same word also means chocolates and sweets.

tuft a small bunch of grass, hair or feathers, growing closely together

tug to pull hard at someone or something

tugboat a small but powerful ship which tows larger ships

tug of war a game in which a team pulls on each end of the same rope. Each team tries to pull the other team over a line.

tulip a brightly-coloured flower with a few large leaves. It grows from a bulb.

tumble to fall over suddenly

tumbler a plain drinking glass with no stem

tummy a pet name for stomach

tune a lot of musical notes played one after the other to make a pretty sound

tunic a close-fitting jacket worn as part of a uniform. The same word also means a loose-fitting belted garment.

tuning-fork a metal instrument with two prongs that give out a musical sound when you strike it

tunnel a hole cut right through a hill or under the ground

turban a long piece of cloth wound round the head and worn as a hat

turbine an engine that works by force of water, steam or gas

turf the top layer of earth with grass growing on it

turkey a big farmyard bird with small wings and a fan-shaped tail

turn to move yourself or some object to the left or the right or all the way round

turning a road branching off a main road to the left or right

turnip the large round root of the turnip plant which can be cooked and eaten

turntable the part of a gramophone or record-player which goes round and round when a record is played

turpentine a kind of oil used in painting. It comes from pine trees.

turret a small tower on a building. The same word also means a revolving platform on a ship or tank that has guns on it.

turtle an animal with a shell, like a tortoise. It has paddle-shaped legs and lives in water.

tusk one of the two very long teeth that stick out of the mouths of some animals such as elephants

tweed a thick, rather rough woollen cloth which is often used to make suits and overcoats

twice two times

twig a little branch on a tree or bush

twilight the fading dim light just before the sun sets

twin one of two children or animals born at the same time to the same mother

twine threads twisted together to make strong string. The same word also means to turn or twist round something.

twinkle to shine and sparkle in flashes, like a star in the sky

twirl to turn round and round very quickly

twist to bend something; to wind one thing around another; to turn sharply

twitter to make a chattering noise, as birds do when a lot of them are together

type to print words on paper by using a typewriter. The same word also means something that belongs to or stands for a group of things, like a type of person or type of food.

typewriter a machine which prints words on paper. It has keys with letters on them which you press.

tyrant a person who rules over people in a cruel way

tyre a rubber ring, usually filled with air, on the outer rim of a car or bicycle wheel

ugly not pretty or pleasant to look at

ukelele a small musical instrument shaped like a guitar

ulcer   an open sore on the skin or inside you

umbrella   a round piece of material stretched over thin pieces of metal. It can be opened and held over your head to keep you from getting wet in the rain.

umpire   someone who settles arguments and decides whether players have broken the rules in games like cricket and tennis

uncle   the brother of your mother or father

uncomfortable   not at ease; feeling awkward

underground   underneath the ground. The same word also means a railway that runs in a tunnel under the ground.

underline   to draw a line under a word

underneath   in a lower place; under something

understand   to know what something means

undo   to unfasten, untie or open something

undone   unfastened; opened

undress   to take your clothes off

unexpected   not expected; sudden

unhappy   not happy; sad

unhealthy   not healthy; sickly

unicorn   an imaginary animal that looks like a horse with a horn in the middle of its forehead

uniform   special clothes worn by those who belong to a group of people such as the army, the navy, or a school

unimportant not important

uninteresting not interesting

union a joining together. The same word also means a group of workers who have joined together.

Union Jack the national flag of the United Kingdom

unit a single thing

unite to join together; to do something together as a group

universal to do with everyone, everywhere

universe all things existing on the earth and out in space

university a place where students who have finished school can go for more education

unkind not kind; cruel

unless if not; if you do not

unlike not like; different

unload to take a load from; to take the bullets out of a gun

unpleasant not pleasant; nasty

unsteady not steady; shaky

unsuccessful not successful; not able to do something you try to do

untidy not neat; not well arranged

until up to the time. You are not allowed to drive a car until you are old enough.

unusual   not usual; out of the ordinary

unwell   ill; not healthy

unwrap   to take the covering off something

up   towards a higher place; the opposite of down

upon   on top of something

uppercut   an upward blow used by a boxer

uproar   a noisy disturbance; shouting and yelling

upset   to knock something over. The same word also means to be worried or ill.

upside-down   turned over, with the top part underneath

upstairs   on a floor above the ground floor of a building

upstream   towards the upper part of a stream

upward   going up

urban   having to do with towns or cities and not the countryside

urge   to try to get someone to do something; to try to persuade

use   to do something with an object made for a special purpose. You use a knife to cut your food.

used   something that is not new

useful   something that is likely to be used a lot; helpful

useless   of no use; of no worth or value

usual happening more often than not

usually almost always; more often than not

vacant empty; not lived in, like a house that people have moved away from

vacation a holiday

vaccinate (*say vaksinate*) to give an injection that will prevent you from getting some diseases

vacuum a space with no air in it

vague not very clear or sure

vain thinking how pretty or good-looking you are; having a very good opinion of yourself

valentine a card or greeting sent to someone you love on Saint Valentine's Day, February 14th

valley the low land between two hills or mountains

valuable worth a lot of money; high-priced: important

value the worth of something; the price or cost of something

van a closed motor vehicle used for carrying things from place to place. The same word also means a special railway carriage used for luggage, mail and animals.

vane a shaped piece of metal on top of a building, that swings to show which way the wind is blowing

vanilla a food flavouring which comes from the dried seed pod of a climbing plant

vanish to go out of sight very quickly; to disappear

vanity too high an opinion of yourself

vapour mist, steam or smoke floating in the air

variety a collection of many kinds of things: a show with different kinds of entertainment

various different; many; several. Ice cream comes in various flavours.

varnish a clear liquid that you paint on to wood and metal to make it look shiny

vase a pretty container for putting flowers in

vast huge; very big; immense

veal the meat from a calf

vegetable any plant used for food

vehicle any form of transport with wheels

veil a thin piece of netting or material, worn by women to hide their faces or to protect them from strong wind or sunshine

vein one of the very thin long tubes that carry the blood around in your body

velvet soft warm material that looks and feels like very thin fur

vengeance revenge

ventilator a small opening in a wall to let stale air out or fresh air in

verandah an open porch with a roof, joined on to a house

verse   poetry; part of a poem

vessel   a ship. The same word also means a
container, usually for liquid.

vest   an undershirt; a waistcoat

vet   a person who looks after sick animals. The
word is short for veterinary surgeon. The same
word also means to examine something to see
that it is all right.

vex   to annoy someone or make him cross

viaduct   a long bridge made to carry a road or
railway over a valley or low-lying area

vicious   wicked; fierce; very spiteful

victim   a person who is hurt in some way or is
killed by someone else's action

victory   the winning of a battle or contest

videotape   a special kind of tape that shows pictures
and gives out sounds when it is played through
a special machine

view   what you can see in front of you. When you
are on top of a hill, you have a good view of
the countryside around the hill.

vigour   strength

viking   a pirate from the north in olden times

village   houses and buildings all together, like a
town but smaller

villain   a bad man; a rogue

vine   a plant that climbs up poles or a fence or
wall or creeps along on the ground. Some vines
have grapes on them.

vinegar   an acid-tasting liquid used in salads and pickles

violent   very rough; forceful

violet   a small wild plant with purple or white flowers

violin   a musical instrument with four strings. It is held under the chin and played with a special stick called a bow.

visible   able to be seen

visibility   the clearness with which things can be seen. In a fog or mist the visibility is bad because you cannot see far.

vision   the ability to see; eyesight

visit   to go to see someone at his house

vitamin   something in foods that is good for you because it keeps you healthy. Milk and oranges both have vitamins that you need.

vivid   very bright; brilliant

vixen   a female fox

vocabulary   all the words you can speak and write: a selected list of words, usually in alphabetical order

voice   the sound that comes from people's mouths when they speak or sing

volcano   a cone-shaped mountain that throws out hot ashes or liquid rock from an opening in the top

volume a book. The same word also means the amount, quantity or bulk of something.

volunteer to offer to do something that you don't have to do

vote to say which person you would choose to be in charge of something or to be a member of a committee or similar group of people

vow a solemn promise

vowel the sounds of a language which are not consonants. Usually vowels are written with the letters *a e i o u.*

voyage a long journey by sea

vulgar rude; not very polite

vulture a large bird of prey that eats dead flesh

wad a bundle of paper, often used for packing

waddle to walk with short steps, rocking from side to side, as a duck does

wade to walk in water

wafer a very thin biscuit

wag to move something up and down or from side to side, as when a dog wags its tail

wage payment for a job of work

wagon an open vehicle with four wheels, used to carry heavy loads

wagtail a small wild bird with a long tail that wags up and down

wail to make a long sad crying noise

waist   the narrow middle part of your body above the hips

waistcoat   a short sleeveless jacket, sometimes worn by men under a coat

wait   to stay in a place until someone comes or something happens

waiter   someone who serves food at a table in a café or restaurant

wake   to become awake after being asleep; to wake up someone who is asleep

walk   to move along on your feet, but more slowly than running

walkie-talkie   a radio carried about with you when you walk, used to send and receive messages

wall   something built of bricks or stone, like the sides of a house or a fence around a garden

wallet   a small pocket case, usually of leather, for carrying paper money, tickets, stamps and personal papers

wallflower   a sweet-smelling garden flower that sometimes grows on old walls

wallop   to hit someone hard

wallpaper   a special kind of paper put on the inside walls of houses as decoration

walnut   a tree which has nuts that are good to eat. The wood is very hard, and is used to make furniture.

walrus   a sea animal, like a large seal with two tusks

wan   pale; looking rather ill or weak

wand   a magic stick used by fairies or by conjurers when they do magic tricks

wander   to roam about from place to place

wane   to become smaller, as when the full moon begins to wane

want   to wish for or to need something

war   a fight between two or more countries. If two groups of people in the same country fight each other, it is called civil war.

ward   a large room in a hospital, where there are a number of beds for sick people

warder   a man who stands guard over prisoners in a prison

wardrobe   a cupboard where you keep clothes

warehouse   a building where goods are stored

warm   more hot than cold

warn   to tell someone to take care because of something that may happen, usually dangerous

warp   to twist out of shape

warrior   a man who fights for his country in time of war; an old-fashioned word for soldier

warship   a ship that has guns and weapons for fighting in a war

wart   a small hard lump on the skin, usually on the hands or face

wash   to make clean, using soap and water

washing   clothes that are being washed or need to
    be washed

wasp   a stinging insect something like a bee with a
    very narrow waist

waste   to use something up or spend money
    carelessly. The same word also means rubbish;
    something of no value that is thrown away.

watch   to look at closely. The same word also
    means a small clock which you wear on your
    wrist or carry in your pocket.

watchful   careful; watching what you are doing

water   the clear liquid in lakes, rivers and seas.
    Water also falls from the clouds as rain.

water closet   a small room containing a bowl which
    has a rushing flow of water to carry away
    waste through a pipe. It is called W.C. for
    short.

watercress   a green plant that grows in fresh water.
    It is eaten in salads and sandwiches.

waterfall   a stream of water falling down from a
    high place

water lily   a water plant with large flat floating
    leaves and beautiful pink, white or yellow
    flowers

waterproof   able to keep water out. A raincoat is
    waterproof.

wave water moving in a curved line on the surface of the sea or a lake. The same word also means to move something, like your hand or a flag, back and forth or up and down.

wavy curving in and out

wax a soft yellowish material used in making candles. The same word also means sealing wax, which melts when you heat it, and then gets hard again.

way a road or path; space to move through. The same word also means how to do something, like the way to paint a picture.

weak not strong

weaken to make something or someone weak

wealth great riches; a lot of money

wean to train a young child or young animal that has been living on milk to eat solid foods

weapon anything used to fight or hunt with, such as a gun, a heavy stick, or a bow and arrows

wear to be dressed in. You wear thin clothes in summer and thick clothes in winter.

weary very tired

weasel a small wild animal with a long slim body. It kills and eats other small animals.

weather what kind of day it is outside. The weather can be wet or dry, hot or cold.

weathercock a flat piece of metal, often in the shape of a cock, that turns in the wind to show you which direction the wind is coming from

weave to make cloth by twisting threads over and under each other

web the lacy net that spiders spin to trap insects

web-foot a foot that has skin joining the toes together. Ducks, geese and swans are all web-footed.

wedding the marriage ceremony, when a man and a woman become husband and wife

wedge a triangular piece of metal or wood, very thin at one end and thicker at the other. You put a wedge between two things to hold them firm or to push them apart.

wee small; tiny

weed wild plants that grow where they are not wanted in gardens or in fields where crops are grown

week seven days

weekend Saturday and Sunday

weep to cry tears

weigh to find out how heavy something is

weight the amount that something weighs

weird strange and frightening

welcome to greet someone with joy

well healthy; properly. The same word also means a deep hole in the ground from which oil or water is obtained.

wellingtons rubber boots

west the direction in which the sun sets; the opposite direction to east

wet   not dry; covered with liquid

whack   to strike something so hard that it makes a noise

whale   the largest animal found in the sea

wharf   a landing place for loading and unloading ships

wheat   a kind of grain from which flour is made

wheel   a large flat circle made of wood or metal. Cars, buses and bicycles must have wheels to be able to move along.

wheelbarrow   a kind of small cart with only one wheel. You carry leaves and grass and building materials in it.

when   at what time; at the time that

whenever   at any time

where   at or in what place

whether   if or if not

whey   the watery part of milk. When cheese is made, the milk is separated into the thick part (called curds) and the liquid part (called whey).

which   one of two or more people or things, as when you decide which friend to invite or which flavour of ice cream you are going to have

whiff   a sudden puff of air, smoke, or scent

while   during the time that; as long as

whimper   to cry in a low whining voice

whine   to make a sad complaining crying sound

whinny   the noise a horse makes by blowing through its nose

whip   a piece of thin strong cord or leather attached to a handle. The same word also means to stir up eggs or cream very quickly.

whirl   to turn round and round very quickly

whisk   to move, sweep or stir something very quickly. The same word also means a kitchen tool used for whipping eggs and cream.

whisker   one of the stiff hairs on a man's face, or at the sides of the mouths of some animals, such as cats, lions and tigers

whisky   a very strong drink made from grain

whisper   to speak so softly that only someone very close to you can hear

whistle   to make a high musical sound by blowing through your mouth with your lips nearly closed. The same word also means a small tube-like instrument that makes a whistling sound when you blow it.

white   the colour of snow

who   which or what person

whole   all; not a part; not divided

whoop   a loud cry or shout. The same word also means the noise made by someone who has the illness called whooping cough.

why   for what reason or cause, as *Why did you go away*?

wick   the twisted threads of cotton in a candle or lamp, which you light

wicked   evil; very bad; the opposite of good

wicket   three stumps in the game of cricket: a small gate or door built into a larger one

wide   a long way from one side to the other; broad; the opposite of narrow

widow   a woman whose husband is dead

widower   a man whose wife is dead

width   how wide or broad something is

wife   a married woman

wig   false hair that you put on over your own hair

wiggly   not straight, like this line $\sim\!\sim\!\sim\!\sim$

wigwam   a tent or hut that American Indians lived in

wild   not kept or looked after by people; the opposite of tame

wilderness   a wild or desert area of land where no one lives

wildflower   a flower that grows without being planted by anyone

wilful   wanting your own way

willing   pleased and ready to do something you are asked to do

willow   a tree with long bending branches and narrow leaves. Cricket bats are usually made of willow wood.

wily   crafty, sly

win   to come first in something, like a race or a game

wind (*rhymes with tinned*)   fast-moving air that blows things about

wind (*rhymes with kind*)   to turn or twist something around, like winding up a ball of string

windmill   a machine that is worked by the wind. It is used for grinding grain or for pumping water.

window   a glass-covered opening in the wall of a building, which lets light and air in

wine   a strong drink made from the juice of grapes

wing   one of the two feathered parts of a bird's body with which it flies. Aeroplanes have metal wings.

wink   to shut and open one eye quickly

winter   the last of the four seasons of the year, when it is coldest

wipe   to clean or dry something by rubbing

wire   a very thin, long piece of metal

wireless   another name for radio, a way of sending sounds through the air without using wires

wise knowing and understanding a lot of things

wish to want something very much

wit understanding, cleverness

witch a wicked, dangerous woman who is supposed to be able to do magic

with near to or alongside. Sometimes the same word also means against, as when you fight with someone.

wither to dry up, to shrivel

within inside; in the inner part

without not having or using something. The same word also means on the outside.

witness someone who has seen something happen and therefore can say he knows all about it

witty clever and amusing

wizard a man who is supposed to be able to do magic

wobble to rock unsteadily from side to side

wolf a dangerous wild animal, that looks like a large dog

woman a female human being; a girl when she is grown up

wonder to be surprised at something marvellous, unexpected or strange. The same word also means to question, to want to know.

wonderful marvellous; amazing

wonderland an imaginary country where amazing and wonderful things happen

wood   a little forest. The same word also means the material that trees are made of. Wood is used to make lots of things like fences, furniture and some buildings.

wooden   made of wood or hard like wood

woodpecker   a wild bird that pecks holes in the bark of trees to find insects for food

woodwork   carpentry; the wooden part of a building or furniture

wool   the thick warm covering of hair on a sheep, which is made into such things as blankets and clothing

woollen   made of wool

word   a spoken sound or group of letters that means something when you hear it or read it

work   to do something useful; not playing

workman   someone who works with his hands, often using tools or machinery

works   a factory or workshop. The same word also means the machinery in something, such as a clock or watch.

world   the earth, the people and things on it, and the air around it

worm   a small snake-like animal which lives underground and moves by wriggling in the earth

worn looking shabby or ragged. Clothes look worn when you have been wearing them for a long time.

worry to be afraid something is going to go wrong or that something bad may happen to someone

worse not so good; more bad

worship to honour and praise God

worst most bad

worth the price you would have to pay for something you want to buy. The same word also means deserving or useful; good enough or valuable enough, as when someone says a book is worth reading.

worthless not worth anything; no good

wound (*rhymes with round*) turned and twisted

wound (*rhymes with spooned*) a cut in your flesh

wrap to cover something by folding paper or cloth around it. The same word also means a shawl or cape worn by girls and women.

wrath great anger

wreath a ring of flowers or leaves twisted together

wreck anything that has been ruined or destroyed, leaving only useless bits and pieces. Sometimes the word is short for shipwreck.

wren a very small brown wild bird

wrest to pull something away from someone by force

wrestle to struggle with someone to see who is stronger

wriggle to move by twisting and turning

wring to make water come out of something, like wet clothes, by twisting and squeezing

wringer a machine with two rollers that wring the water out of wet washing

wrinkle a small fold or crease in material, cloth, paper or the skin of old people

wrist the thin part of your arm that joins on to your hand

write to draw letters or words so that people can read them

writhe to wriggle or twist about

writing something you have written

wrong not right; evil or wicked

x-ray a special kind of photograph which shows doctors what the inside of your body looks like

xylophone a set of narrow pieces of wood that make musical sounds when they are hit with wooden hammers

yacht (*rhymes with got*) a kind of boat, usually with sails, used for racing or for pleasure

yak a long-haired ox

yap to bark sharply

yard a space, usually closed in by buildings or a fence. The same word also means a measurement of 36 inches or 3 feet.

yarn thread made from wool or cotton. The same word also means a story told by someone who has travelled a lot.

yawn to open your mouth wide and breathe air in and out slowly, especially when you are sleepy or bored

year a length of time; 365 days, 52 weeks or 12 months make a year.

yell to call out very loudly

yellow a colour. Lemons and primroses are yellow and so are the yolks of eggs.

yelp a short sharp cry or bark

yes the word you use to show you agree

yesterday the day before today

yet by now. The same word sometimes also means but.

yew an evergreen tree, often seen growing in churchyards

yield to give up, as when the enemy surrenders. The same word also means to produce, as when a field of wheat yields a good crop.

yogurt slightly sour thick milk, often mixed with a fruity flavouring. The word is sometimes spelled yoghurt or yoghourt.

yolk the yellow part in the middle of an egg

yonder over there; beyond

young   not old; in the early part of life

younger   not as old as someone else

youngster   a young person who is not yet grown up

yourself   you and no one else

youth   the time when you are young. The same
word also means a young man.

yo-yo   a toy in the shape of a reel, which spins up
and down on a string

zebra   a wild animal like a small horse with stripes

zero   nothing

zest   joy in what you are doing; enthusiasm

zigzag   moving from side to side, like this line

zinc   a bluish-white metal

zip   a long metal or plastic fastener used to do up
clothing and to close purses and bags

zipper   another word for zip-fastener

zither a musical instrument made of a flat board with lots of metal strings stretched across it. You pluck the strings to make musical sounds.

zone a large area of the world which is different from other areas because, for example, it has a much hotter or much colder climate

zoo a place where wild animals are kept and people can come to look at them. The word is short for zoological gardens.